Open Forum

ACADEMIC LISTENING AND SPEAKING

2

OXFORD
UNIVERSITY PRESS

UNIVERSITY PRESS

198 Madison Avenue
New York, NY 10016 USA

Great Clarendon Street, Oxford ox2 6dp UK

Oxford University Press is a department of the University of Oxford.
It furthers the University's objective of excellence in research, scholarship,
and education by publishing worldwide in

Oxford New York

Auckland Cape Town Dar es Salaam Hong Kong Karachi
Kuala Lumpur Madrid Melbourne Mexico City Nairobi
New Delhi Shanghai Taipei Toronto

With offices in

Argentina Austria Brazil Chile Czech Republic France Greece
Guatemala Hungary Italy Japan Poland Portugal Singapore
South Korea Switzerland Thailand Turkey Ukraine Vietnam

OXFORD and OXFORD ENGLISH are registered trademarks of
Oxford University Press

© Oxford University Press 2006

Database right Oxford University Press (maker)

Library of Congress Cataloging-in-Publication Data

Blackwell, Angela.
  Open Forum. Intermediate / Angela M. Blackwell, Therese Naber.
    p. cm.
Includes bibliographical references.
isbn: 978-0-19-436111-8 (student book)
isbn: 978-0-19-436112-5 (audio cd component)
isbn: 978-0-19-441777-8 (audio cassette component)
isbn: 978-0-19-441775-4 (answer key and test packet)
  1. English language—Textbooks for foreign speakers. I. Title: Open Forum
intermediate. II. Naber, Therese. III. Title.
PE1128.B5844 2006
428.3'4—dc22   2005030682

No unauthorized photocopying

All rights reserved. No part of this publication may be reproduced,
stored in a retrieval system, or transmitted, in any form or by any means,
without the prior permission in writing of Oxford University Press,
or as expressly permitted by law, or under terms agreed with the appropriate
copyright clearance organization. Enquiries concerning reproduction outside
the scope of the above should be sent to the ELT Rights Department, Oxford
University Press, at the address above.

You must not circulate this book in any other binding or cover
and you must impose this same condition on any acquirer.

Any websites referred to in this publication are in the public domain and
their addresses are provided by Oxford University Press for information only.
Oxford University Press disclaims any responsibility for the content.

Executive Publisher: Janet Aitchison
Senior Acquisitions Editor: Pietro Alongi
Editor: Jeff Holt
Associate Editor: Scott Allan Wallick
Art Director: Maj-Britt Hagsted
Art Editor: Justine Eun
Production Manager: Shanta Persaud
Production Controller: Eve Wong

isbn: 978 0 19 436111 8

Printed in Hong Kong.

10 9 8 7 6 5 4

Photo Credits:
*The publishers would like to thank the following for their permission to reproduce
photographs:*
Alamy: Bill Bachmann, 35 (tourists); Blend Images, 101 (bowing);
Andrew Holt, 83 (tutor); imageshop-zefa media uk ltd, 35 (bridge);
Butch Martin, 35 (graduates); Chris McLennan, 28 (man painting);
mediacolor's, 83 (lecture); POPPERFOTO, 93; J. Schwanke, 100
(observatory); Stephen Frick Collection, 38 (toadfish); Penny Tweedie, 28
(woman with painting); Ardea London LTD: Francois Gohier, 38 (whale);
Art Resource, NY: Bridgeman-Giraudon, 30; Classett: Brand X Pictures,
10 (basketball); Ingram Publishing, 38 (skatefish); Photodisc, 5, 23 (fast
food), 51 (house painter); CORBIS: Bettman, 69; Getty Images: Donna
Day/Stone, 73 (TV); The Hemera Collection: 18, 23 (dinner plate), 27
(mask, statue), 31, 38 (horshoe crab, coral, snail), 64, 97; Suzy Hwang:
101 (school uniforms); Indexstock: Stewart Cohen, 51 (home office);
John Dominis, 42; The Fringe, 27 (painting); Jim McGuire, 10 (reading);
Erwin Bud Nielsen, 37 (marine biologist); Reprinted by permission of
the Modern Language Association, 57; NASA: NASA Headquarters—
GReatest Images of NASA (NASA-HQ-GRIN), 100 (space shuttle); NASA
Marshall Space Flight Center (NASA-MSFC), 100 (space probe); Omni-
Photo Communications: Visual&Written, 73 (Time Square); OUP: Justine
Eun, 72; Project for Public Spaces, Inc. www.pps.org: 7; Punchstock:
Bananastock, 80, 109; Stockbyte Platinum, 37 (doctor); Kathy Rose
Sargent: 27 (child's art).

Art Credits:
Annie Bissett: 1, 8, 10, 18, 46, 56, 73, 77, 93

Acknowledgements

We would like to acknowledge Janet Aitchison and Pietro Alongi, who initiated the *Open Forum* series. We would also like to thank the editors—Jeffrey Holt and Scott Allan Wallick—and the design team at OUP for their hard work and dedication throughout the project. We would also like to express our gratitude to the following people for their support and feedback during the development of the series: Nigel Caplan, Jack Crow, Barbara Mattingly, and Adrianne Ochoa.

The publisher would like to thank the Hirshhorn Museum and Sculpture Garden, Smithsonian Institution, for permission to reproduce the following work:

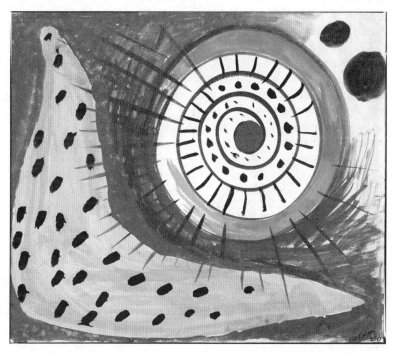

Spiral Composition, 1946

Alexander Calder (1898–1976)

Gouache on paper (44.8 x 50.7 cm)

Hirshhorn Museum and Sculpture Garden, Smithsonian Institution, Gift of Joseph H. Hirshhorn, 1966.

Photographer: Lee Stalsworth.

Contents

Contents   **v**

Introduction

Welcome to *Open Forum*, a three-level listening and speaking skills series for English language learners who need practice in extended listening and discussion in preparation for academic work, or to attain a personal goal.

The series is structured around high-interest listening texts with an academic focus that engage and motivate learners. Chapters feature academic content areas such as business, history, or psychology. The content areas are revisited as the series progresses, ensuring that learners recycle and extend the ideas and vocabulary of each topic. Focused practice in listening and speaking skills is integrated into each chapter.

Open Forum 2 is for students at the **intermediate** level.

Features of *Open Forum*

Listening Skills

- Each chapter introduces and practices a specific listening skill (e.g., listening for main points, identifying opinions and supporting arguments).
- Listening selections are adapted from authentic sources. They are carefully chosen to engage learners and teachers and to stimulate discussion.
- A wide variety of texts—including lectures, radio interviews, news reports, and informal conversations—ensures learners practice listening to a range of audio formats.
- Listening comprehension tasks provide opportunities for extensive and intensive listening, which becomes more challenging as learners progress through the series.

Speaking Skills

- Each chapter introduces and practices one specific speaking skill (e.g., explaining a process, managing a conversation).
- Speaking practice sections in each chapter provide opportunities for extended discussion on the chapter theme.
- Abundant opportunities for interaction in pairs, groups, and as a class ensure student participation.

Vocabulary

- Vocabulary sections introduce key lexical items associated with the chapter theme. The sections also highlight word-building, collocations, and phrasal verbs.

Pronunciation

- Pronunciation sections raise learners' awareness of features of natural spoken English (e.g., intonation with questions, linking).

MP3 Component

- Downloadable audio files (in MP3 format) for each chapter are available on the *Open Forum* Web site, www.oup.com/elt/openforum. Each selection complements the topic in the corresponding chapter, and provides learners with opportunities for extended listening practice in the content areas. The listening selections can be used independently or in a language lab setting.

Assessment

- Progress Tests (available in the *Answer Key and Test Booklet*) enable teachers to check learners' progress and allow learners to demonstrate mastery of the strategies they have studied.

Unit Format

1. Introducing the Topic

This section introduces the topic of the chapter, activates learners' background knowledge, and builds interest. Learners complete a quiz, answer discussion questions, look at photographs, or complete a survey.

Teaching Tip: Use this section to get students thinking and speaking about the chapter theme. Have them work in pairs or groups to maximize their speaking opportunities.

2. Listening Practice

This is the first of two major listening opportunities in each chapter. Each listening section includes five subsections:

- **Preparing to Listen**

  Here learners are given specific preparation for the text that they are going to hear. Learners read and discuss information specific to the piece; at this point, new vocabulary may be introduced to facilitate listening.

  Teaching Tip: Heighten student interest and anticipation by having them predict what speakers will say. Leave some questions unanswered; this will motivate students to listen more carefully.

- **Listening for Main Ideas**

  This stage ensures that learners are able to identify the main idea of a text. The listening task encourages learners to listen to the entire recording once through, without stopping, and to pick out the general gist of the text.

  Teaching Tip: Read through the directions for the task before learners listen. Check that they understand the vocabulary in the task and know what they have to do. Encourage them to focus only on the listening task as they listen. After they listen, have learners compare their answers, and check as a class.

- **Listening for More Detail**

  In this section, learners practice listening for specific details. As the series progresses, learners move from reacting with a minimal response (e.g., deciding whether a statement is true or false) to making more extended notes (e.g., filling in a chart). They are guided to use context to work out unknown vocabulary.

  Teaching Tip: Go through the questions before learners listen, and check that they understand what they are being asked. Then play the recording. Learners may already be able to answer some of the questions. Acknowledge this fact, but do not confirm right or wrong answers at this point: encourage learners to listen a second time to check their answers. After they have listened again, ask students to compare their answers, and check as a class. If learners have difficulty with one or more of the questions, replay the relevant section of the recording as necessary.

- **Thinking and Speaking**

  At this point, learners are encouraged to respond to the ideas in the text, synthesize what they have heard, and apply it to their own experience. Learners also get an opportunity for speaking practice on the chapter theme.

  Teaching Tip: Learners can discuss the questions in pairs, small groups, or as a class. Give them time to think before asking for answers. Encourage them to refer to the listening transcript if appropriate. The tasks are designed to be flexible and can take as little as a few minutes, or as long as 20–30 minutes, depending on class and teacher preference.

- **Focus on the Listening Skill**

  This section raises learners' awareness of listening skills and strategies, and provides focused training in those skills. The *Listening Skill* boxes introduce three types of listening skills:

  a. pre-listening skills (e.g., previewing vocabulary) are introduced before learners listen to the text;

  b. while-listening skills (e.g., identifying main points) are introduced and practiced as learners listen;

  c. detailed listening skills (e.g., working out unknown vocabulary) are practiced after students have grasped the main points.

  Teaching Tip: Read the information in the Listening Skill *box aloud as the learners follow along. Check that they understand. Then have them complete the tasks alone or with a partner. After they listen, have learners compare their answers, and check as a class.*

3. ## Vocabulary

   The vocabulary section introduces key items of vocabulary that are useful for the topic, and provides written and oral practice of the items. Where necessary, *FYI* boxes highlight relevant information.

   Teaching Tip: Read the information in the FYI box, if there is one, aloud as the learners follow along.

Check that learners understand. Then ask learners to complete the tasks alone or with a partner.

4. ## Listening Practice

   This section provides a second listening opportunity. The text in this section is longer than the first text, to give learners practice in extended listening. The text is usually of a different type from the first text (e.g., a lecture vs. a radio interview). The sequence of tasks is the same as in the first listening section, without the specific focus on a listening skill.

   Teaching Tip: See previous Listening Practice.

5. ## Pronunciation

   Learners are offered practice in listening for and understanding features of naturally spoken English (e.g., stress, linking, weak forms, and verb endings). Learners practice focused listening to identify stress and intonation and to pick out words and complete sentences. As in the *Vocabulary* section, *FYI* boxes provide relevant instruction.

   Teaching Tip: Read the information in the FYI box, if there is one, aloud as the learners follow along. Check that learners understand. Then, ask learners to complete the tasks alone or with a partner.

6. ## Speaking Skills

   This section raises learners' awareness of a specific speaking skill or strategy, such as asking for clarification or hesitating. These are presented in *Speaking Skill* boxes. Learners listen to a short text that exemplifies the skill or strategy in question.

   Teaching Tip: Read the information in the Speaking Skill *box aloud as the learners follow along. Check that students understand. Then, ask learners to complete the tasks alone or with partner.*

7. ## Speaking Practice

   This section provides an extensive, guided speaking activity on the theme of the chapter, and encourages students to use the skill learned in the previous section. The activity is carefully staged to maximize speaking; for example, learners might first make notes individually, then discuss the topic with a partner, and finally move into group or class discussion.

   Teaching Tip: Allow plenty of time for this activity. Ask students to gather and note down their ideas; this will ensure that they have enough to say in the speaking stage. If necessary, remind learners to use the speaking skill from the previous section.

8. ## Taking Skills Further

   The chapter concludes with suggestions to increase learners' awareness of listening and speaking skills, and ideas for listening and speaking practice outside the classroom.

   Teaching Tip: The task can usually be checked in the next class. Many of the activities can be expanded into a project, if desired.

ABOUT THIS CHAPTER

Topic:	City planning
Listening Texts:	Lecture about city planning; interview about planning public parks
Listening Skill Focus:	Activating background knowledge
Speaking Skill Focus:	Reflecting on speaking
Vocabulary:	Compound nouns
Pronunciation:	Sentence stress

1 INTRODUCING THE TOPIC

1. Complete the survey. Then compare your answers as a class. What are your top three necessities?

What's important in choosing a place to live?

Check the box that best describes your opinion.

	Not at all Important	Not very Important	Somewhat Important	Very Important
1. A large house with a spacious yard				
2. A sense of being "away from it all"				
3. A commute of 45 minutes or less				
4. Being close to a highway				
5. Walking distance to public transportation				
6. Sidewalks and places to take walks				
7. A community with a mix of older and younger people				
8. A community with a mix of people from different backgrounds				

2. With a partner, look at the published results of the survey. Does your class have the same priorities as the people who took the survey?

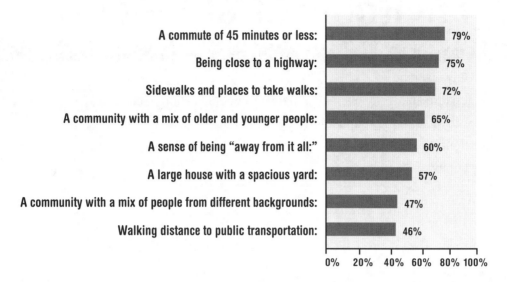

A commute of 45 minutes or less: 79%
Being close to a highway: 75%
Sidewalks and places to take walks: 72%
A community with a mix of older and younger people: 65%
A sense of being "away from it all:" 60%
A large house with a spacious yard: 57%
A community with a mix of people from different backgrounds: 47%
Walking distance to public transportation: 46%

0% 20% 40% 60% 80% 100%

2 | LISTENING PRACTICE

A Preparing to Listen

1. You are about to listen to a lecture on the topic of city planning. Read the description of the talk.

> ## 3:30 Lecture: City Planning
>
> **Description:** One of the most serious problems facing America's towns and cities has been the decline of inner cities alongside the growth of suburbs. A city planner describes the causes of this decline and discusses a new approach to development that aims to revitalize our cities and make them more attractive places to live.

2. Work with a partner. For each of the following items, find a word in the description that has the same meaning.

   1. The building of houses, streets, and so on, in an area: _development_

   2. Residential areas outside the central part of a city: _____

   3. Central areas of a large city that often have a lot of social problems: _____

4. The process of becoming weaker or less healthy: _____

5. To bring life back to a place: _____

B Focus on the Listening Skill: Activating Background Knowledge

> **LISTENING SKILL**
>
> Before you listen to a talk on a particular topic, think about what you already know about the subject and brainstorm some words and expressions that are connected to the topic. This is a useful way to prepare for listening, even if the words and expressions are not actually used in the talk.

1. Think about the topic of the talk: revitalizing inner cities. Discuss the following questions with a partner.

   1. Why might some U.S. inner cities need to be revitalized?

   2. How do you think it might be possible to revitalize the inner cities?

2. Now brainstorm some words that are connected to the topic. Then compare lists with your partner.

   development _____

   _____

   _____

   _____

   _____

   _____

   _____

   _____

C Listening for Main Ideas

Listen to the lecture. As you listen, number the topics in the order that they are discussed.

_____ a. The characteristics of smart growth

_____ b. The decline of the inner cities

_____ c. The growth of the suburbs

_____ d. The role of city planners

D Listening for More Detail

Listen again. For each item, choose the correct sentence ending according to the lecture. Then compare answers with a partner. Listen again if necessary.

1. America's inner cities have been in a bad state for _____.
   a. 30–50 years
   b. about 100 years

2. Inner cities declined because _____.
   a. people moved to the suburbs
   b. the downtown stores weren't of high quality

3. Many towns are losing their cultural life because _____.
   a. people aren't interested in culture
   b. people don't want to go downtown at night

4. It's important to revitalize the inner cities because _____.
   a. people want to live closer to their jobs
   b. people don't like the suburbs

5. Diversity of use helps to revitalize a neighborhood because _____.
   a. people can live near their jobs
   b. it brings people to a neighborhood throughout the day

6. Housing diversity is a good thing because _____.
   a. it attracts different age and income levels
   b. communities should provide affordable housing

7. City planners now prefer to locate schools and stores _____.
   a. away from residential areas
   b. close to residential areas

8. Attractive outdoor spaces are good for a community because _____.
   a. they encourage people to come out to the streets
   b. they make people feel better

E Thinking and Speaking

1. Work with a partner. Choose one of the following topics, and explain what the speaker said about it. Use your own words, and give details.

   • How inner cities declined

   • Diversity of use and why it is important

   • Diversity of housing and why it is important

2. Think of an area where you live that has changed in some way. How has development (or lack of development) helped or not helped the area? Use the following items as examples. Discuss in small groups.

A neighborhood that has declined

A place where there is a lot of new housing

A neighborhood that is being revitalized

An outdoor space that has become more attractive

3 VOCABULARY: Compound Nouns

A compound noun is created by putting together two or more nouns. The first noun acts like an adjective. For example, a *shopping area* is an *area* where there is *shopping*. A *tourist attraction* is an *attraction* for *tourists*.

1. Underline seven more compound nouns in the following extract from a guidebook.

SEEING *the* CITY

There are many notable buildings in the business district. City Hall and the Opera House are both fine examples of classical architecture, and are worth a visit. From there, it's a short walk to the main shopping area of the city where there are several large department stores and sidewalk cafés. Since the traffic can be slow, especially at rush hour, consider taking the subway. The nearest subway station is 24th Street.

2. Form six more compound nouns by matching a word from the first column with a word from the second column.

1. tourist _____attraction_____   a. building

2. shopping _____   b. ~~attraction~~

3. bus _____   c. market

4. office _____   d. park

5. ball _____   e. stop

6. produce _____   f. mall

3. Work with a partner. Imagine a friend is interested in coming to live in your town or city. Describe your town or city in terms of the following features. Use words from exercise 2 on the previous page.

Features of a Town or City
The inner-city and the suburbs
Traffic management and public transportation
Shopping and leisure
Tourist attractions

4 | LISTENING PRACTICE

A Preparing to Listen

1. You are going to hear an interview with an expert on planning public parks. Work in small groups and answer the following questions.

   1. What do you think an expert on planning public parks does? _____

   _____

   2. What decisions might he or she have to make? _____

   _____

   3. What words and expressions are connected to the topic "planning public parks"?

   _____

   _____

2. Compare answers with a partner. For item 3, did you think of the same words?

B Listening for Main Ideas

Listen to the interview. As you listen, check the three features that are discussed.

_____ a. activities

_____ b. trees and plants

_____ c. seating

_____ d. entrances and paths

_____ e. monuments

C Listening for More Detail

 Read the questions below. Then listen to the interview again. As you listen, note your answers to the questions. Then compare answers with a partner. Listen again if necessary.

1. How does Mr. Ong describe an unsuccessful public park?

2. What attractions in Central Park does he mention?

3. Why is it a good idea to connect activities to each other?

4. What always attracts people?

5. What kinds of users mean that a park is successful?

6. What problems with seating does Mr. Ong mention?

7. Why should the interior of a park be visible from the outside?

8. What kinds of paths does Mr. Ong *not* like?

D Thinking and Speaking

Each of these photographs of public spaces shows a problem described in the interview. Using the information you heard in the interview, discuss what the problem is in each photograph and how you think it could be solved.

5 PRONUNCIATION: Sentence Stress

FYI Speakers stress the words that are most important in an argument. This helps listeners understand the main points.

1. Read and listen to this extract. Note how the speaker stresses the words that are most important.

Central Park, in **New York**, for example, is a **great** park. There's a lot to **do** there. You've got several **museums** right around it, and in the park **itself** you have the Children's **Zoo**, you have an outdoor **theater**, you have a **skating** rink, **lots** of playgrounds, **community** centers, and so on—**all** of that **brings** people **in**.

2. Now listen to this extract and underline the stressed words. Compare answers with a partner.

> For example, let's say you have a park with a playground in one corner, and a fountain in the middle. Well, that's nice, but there's not enough there to attract people. But if you link the two together—say you make a water feature in the playground, or you make the fountain safe so that kids can play in it in the summer—and if you add some good seating where people can watch both areas, then you provide more reasons for people to go there.

3. Read one or both of the extracts aloud, stressing the key words.

6 SPEAKING PRACTICE

1. Work with a partner. Have your partner close his or her book. Look at the plan of park A and describe the plan so that your partner can draw it. Then reverse roles and use the plan for park B. Here are some useful expressions you might want to use:

in the top right/left corner   next to

in the bottom right/left corner   across from

in the northeast/southwest, etc., corner   facing

in the middle   leading from . . . to . . .

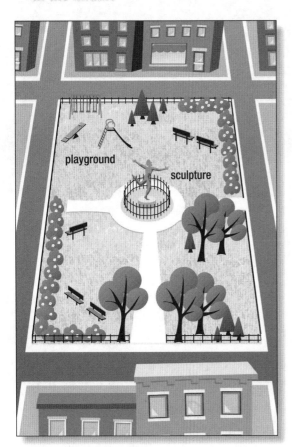

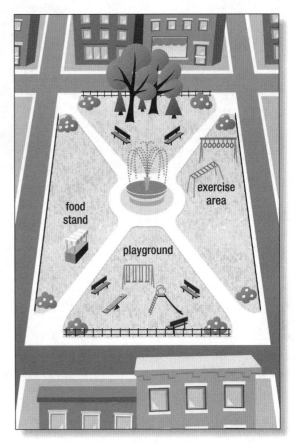

2. Discuss the two plans with your partner. Which plan do you think would be more successful? Why?

7 | SPEAKING SKILLS: Reflecting on Speaking

SPEAKING SKILL

Think about your experiences and needs with speaking. This will help you identify the areas you need to work on, set some goals for your learning, and monitor your own progress.

1. Look at these comments from language learners describing their experiences with speaking. Add one of your own.

1. I sometimes only answer with *yes* or *no* when I feel I should say more.

4. I don't know what to say if I haven't understood what the other person has said.

6. I get *really* nervous when I have to give presentations in class!

2. I get stuck when I don't remember the exact word that I need.

5. It's hard for me to participate in a group discussion.

7. Your comment:
_____
_____
_____
_____

3. I find it hard to express my opinions.

2. Work in small groups. Discuss the comments and compare your own experiences with speaking. Have you experienced any of these problems?

3. In this book, you will have the opportunity to practice speaking by discussing a wide range of topics in pairs or groups. You will also learn some language and strategies to help you with speaking. For example, in Chapter 2 you will practice ways to elaborate, or say more, in response to a question (see comment 1 above). Look at the list of speaking skills in the Table of Contents at the front of the book. Which chapters might help with which of the problems above?

8 | TAKING SKILLS FURTHER

Talk to someone outside of class who is learning to speak another language. Ask them about their difficulties with speaking. How are your experiences similar or different? Discuss your findings in the next class.

 For additional listening practice on the topic of city planning, go to the *Open Forum* Web site (www.oup.com/elt/openforum) and follow the links.

Topics:	Leisure activities; quality of life
Listening Texts:	Radio program about the concept of "flow"; personal interviews
Listening Skill Focus:	Reflecting on listening
Focus:	Elaborating to keep a conversation going
Vocabulary:	Word building with noun suffixes
Pronunciation:	Unstressed function words

1 INTRODUCING THE TOPIC

1. Look at these results of a survey asking the question "What are your favorite leisure-time activities?" Then discuss the questions below with a partner.

Favorite Leisure-Time Activities for Adults in the United States

Favorite Activity	1995	2000	2004
Reading	28%	31%	35%
Watching TV	25%	23%	21%
Spending time with family	12%	14%	20%
Going to movies	8%	6%	10%
Fishing	10%	9%	8%
Computer activities	2%	6%	7%
Walking	8%	8%	6%
Exercise (aerobics, weights)	2%	6%	6%
Playing team sports	9%	5%	5%

SOURCE: HarrisInteractive, the Harris Poll #97, December 8, 2004

1. Are there any activities that you are surprised to see on the list?

2. Which activities have increased in popularity over time? Which have decreased in popularity? What reasons might there be for these changes?

3. Which activities do you think will change in popularity in the future?

4. What other leisure activities can you think of?

2. Work with a partner. Answer the questions about the activities in exercise 1. Then compare your answers in small groups.

    1. Which activities are physical?

    _____

    2. Which activities require concentration?

    _____

    3. Which activities are usually done with other people?

    _____

    4. Which activities are solitary?

    _____

3. Do you think certain types of activities (for example, those that are more physical or more solitary) make better pastimes? Why or why not?

2   LISTENING PRACTICE

A   Preparing to Listen

1. Discuss these questions with a partner.

    1. What do you think "quality of life" means? Does it have to do only with money, or are there other factors involved?

    2. Make a list of things (activities, experiences, etc.) that you think contribute to quality of life.

2. Compare lists as a class. How similar or different are your lists?

B   Listening for Main Ideas

Listen to the radio program. Then complete each statement with the correct ending.

    1. Flow is described by a psychologist as a state of _____.
      a. optimal experience
      b. deep relaxation

    2. A person can experience flow during _____.
      a. one or two types of activities only
      b. many different activities

    3. Flow is _____.
      a. the same as feeling happy
      b. different from feeling happy

C Listening for More Detail

Listen again. Write *T* for true or *F* for false for each statement.

_____ 1. The concept of flow was described by a psychologist.

_____ 2. The psychologist describes being a chef in a restaurant to explain flow.

_____ 3. It is typical to lose a sense of time and to forget your problems when experiencing flow.

_____ 4. Both skill and challenge are required to experience flow.

_____ 5. You can experience flow in both physical and nonphysical activities.

_____ 6. According to the speaker, watching TV is sometimes likely to produce flow.

_____ 7. Reading is not a typical activity that produces flow.

_____ 8. It is possible to feel happy without experiencing flow.

D Thinking and Speaking

Work in small groups. Discuss these questions.

1. Do you think you have ever experienced flow? If so, during what activities?

2. Do you agree with the psychologist that this kind of experience might be important for achieving quality of life? Why or why not?

E Focus on the Listening Skill: Reflecting on Listening

> **LISTENING SKILL**
>
> It is helpful to think about what skills are necessary to be a good listener and to practice them as much as possible. This will improve your skills and make you feel more confident when listening.

1. Here are some comments from language learners who are describing their experiences with listening to lectures, stories, etc. Add a comment of your own. Then discuss the comments in small groups and compare your experiences with listening.

1. It's difficult to understand the beginning of lectures, especially when I'm not prepared or haven't thought about the topic.

3. I panic if I don't recognize a word when I'm listening. I wish I was better at figuring out words I don't know.

5. I don't always understand the point of a story or example.

2. Sometimes it's hard to tell which points are the main points in a lecture.

4. I get nervous if there are a lot of numbers in a lecture. I'm afraid I'll miss some important information.

6. Your comment:

_____

_____

2. In this book, you will have the opportunity to practice different skills and strategies to help you improve your listening abilities. For example, in Chapter 1 you listened to a lecture and a radio interview and practiced activating background knowledge. Look at the list of listening skills in the Table of Contents. Which chapters might help you with the problems mentioned in exercise 1?

3 | VOCABULARY: Word Building with Noun Suffixes

1. You can form nouns from verbs by adding the suffixes *-ion*, *-ation*, and *-ment*. Look at the following sentences and underline the suffixes. What happens to the *e* at the end of the word when you add *-ation* or *-ion*?

    1. People say they experience deep feelings of concentration and enjoyment.

    2. Many people experience relaxation.

2. Complete the following chart with the noun forms of the verbs on the left. Use the suffix indicated.

verb	noun (with *-ion*)	verb	noun (with *-ation*)	verb	noun (with *-ment*)
concentrate	concentration	relax	relaxation	enjoy	enjoyment
connect		prepare		require	
contribute		combine		retire	
discuss		organize		develop	
motivate		explore		manage	
participate				achieve	

3. Fill in the blank with the singular or plural noun form of the words in italics.

    1. I go fishing to help me *relax*. What do you do for _____?

    2. Kelly wants to make a _____ to charity. Do you want to *contribute*?

    3. Have you *discussed* the problem with anyone? I'd be happy to have a _____ with you.

    4. Isabel is very *motivated* to learn. Do you have a lot of _____ to learn?

    5. Paul has *achieved* a lot in his field. Linda also has many _____ in her field.

    6. Do you need to *prepare* a lot for dinner? I can help you with the _____.

7. Biology is a *required* class for my degree. Is biology a _____ for your degree?

8. Did Chong *indicate* his feelings to you? He gave me no _____ at all.

4 LISTENING PRACTICE

A Preparing to Listen

Discuss these questions in pairs or groups.

1. What different kinds of surveys do you know of (e.g., telephone, door-to-door)? What is the information typically used for (e.g., marketing)?

2. Have you ever participated in a survey? If so, what kind was it and what was it for?

3. Look at this part of a survey. What do you think the purpose of the survey is?

Quality-of-Life Survey

Please rate the levels of motivation, concentration, and enjoyment you get from each of the following activities (1 = lowest level, 5 = highest level).

	Motivation	Concentration	Enjoyment	Total
1. Working				
2. Studying				

B Listening for Main Ideas

Listen to the personal interviews about some results of the survey on quality of life. Write two things that each person enjoys.

1. Julia: _____ _____

2. Leo: _____ _____

3. Annie: _____ _____

4. Robert: _____ _____

C Listening for More Detail

Listen to the conversations again. Circle the correct word or phrase to complete each statement.

Julia

1. She has about (an hour and a half/a half-hour) drive to and from work.

2. She likes to (listen to the radio or music/have silence) when she drives.

3. She plays the guitar at least (three times/four times) a week.

4. She plays (with friends and alone/only with friends).

Leo

1. He says there is (a lot of/very little) difference between work and play for him.

2. He (plays computer games/watches TV) when he is not working.

3. He is developing a new (software program/computer game) with a friend.

4. He (likes/doesn't like) socializing.

Annie

1. She enjoys (a few/many) sports.

2. She participates in (team and individual sports/team sports only).

3. She likes her work as a (coach/teacher) more.

4. She (never/sometimes) watches TV in the evening.

Robert

1. He likes doing dishes because it's (relaxing/an unusual activity).

2. He often (plans his day/finds solutions to problems) while washing dishes.

3. He has a job that (is stressful/he loves).

4. On weekends, he (brings office work home/enjoys bicycling).

D Thinking and Speaking

Work in small groups and discuss these questions:

1. Whose response is most surprising?

2. Which person is most similar to you?

3. What do you think the information in this survey could be used for?

5 PRONUNCIATION: Unstressed Function Words

FYI Some very common words, such as articles (*a, an, the*), prepositions (*to, for, of, on, from, at, in*), and conjunctions (*and, or, as, than*) are usually unstressed in both formal and informal speech. They can be difficult to hear because they are unstressed.

 1. Read this part of Julia's response. Circle the words that you think will be unstressed. Compare answers with a partner. Then listen to the response and check your answers.

I usually play the guitar at least three times a week. I play in a group with friends, and I play by myself, too.

🎧 2. Listen to this part of Robert's response, and fill in the missing words. Compare answers with a partner and listen again if necessary.

I'm (1) ___an___ executive with (2) _____ high-pressure job. I'm busy all

(3) _____ time, (4) _____ I like doing dishes? But, it's relaxing

(5) _____ me, (6) _____ it often turns out (7) _____ be good thinking

time. I'm surprised (8) _____ how often I come up (9) _____ solutions

(10) _____ problems while I'm washing dishes.

6 SPEAKING SKILLS: Elaborating to Keep a Conversation Going

SPEAKING SKILL

Good speakers usually elaborate, or say more than just "Yes" or "No," in response to a question. This helps keep the conversation going.

🎧 1. Listen to an extract from Annie's conversation. How does she respond to the interviewer? Does she say only "Yes" or "No," or does she say more? Why is this type of response important?

2. Look at these questions and answers. Think of ways to elaborate on the answers. Then practice asking and answering the questions with a partner.

1. Do you like sports?

   Yes/No, _____.

2. Do you watch TV a lot?

   Yes/No, _____.

3. Do you read books or magazines a lot?

   Yes/No, _____.

4. Are you a good cook?

   Yes/No, _____.

5. Can you fix cars or other machines?

   Yes/No, _____.

6. Do you like using computers and the Internet?

   Yes/No, _____.

7 SPEAKING PRACTICE

1. Complete the quality-of-life survey below. Then work with a partner and take turns interviewing each other about the results. When responding to questions, remember to elaborate—don't just respond with "Yes" or "No". Take notes about your partner's answers.

Quality-of-Life Survey

Please rate the levels of motivation, concentration, and enjoyment you get from each of the following activities (1 = lowest level, 5 = highest level).

	Motivation	Concentration	Enjoyment	Total
1. Working				
2. Studying				
3. Driving				
4. Doing housework (Name the work)				
5. Doing a hobby (Specify)				
6. Doing sports (Specify)				
7. Watching sports				
8. Socializing				
9. Other (Specify)				

2. Compare the survey results in small groups. Can you make any generalizations about the results?

8 TAKING SKILLS FURTHER

Outside of class, pay attention to conversations between native speakers. Notice how people respond to *Yes/No* questions. In what situations do they elaborate? What effect do different types of responses have on a conversation? Compare your findings in the next class.

For additional listening practice on the topic of psychology, go to the *Open Forum* Web site (www.oup.com/elt/openforum) and follow the links.

Topics:	Food; changes in habits
Listening Texts:	Lecture about taste in food; interview with a food scientist
Listening Skill Focus:	Predicting
Speaking Skill Focus:	Hesitating and taking time to think
Vocabulary:	Verbs + *-ing* form or infinitive
Pronunciation:	Intonation with questions

1 | INTRODUCING THE TOPIC

1. Work with a partner. Read the quiz and discuss possible answers. (The answers are at the bottom of the page.)

Food Quiz

1 The largest producer of sugar in the world is ———.

   a. Mexico
   b. Brazil

2 The consumption of sugar worldwide is ———.

   a. going up
   b. going down

3 Tomatoes are officially ———.

   a. a fruit
   b. a vegetable

4 Potatoes originally came from ———.

   a. Europe
   b. South America

5 The most widely grown crop in the world is———.

   a. citrus fruit
   b. wheat

6 Per year, each person in the United States eats about ——— of citrus fruit.

   a. 8 pounds
   b. 12 pounds

7 Per year, the average person in the United States consumes about ——— of coffee.

   a. 3 pounds
   b. 9 pounds

8 The highest consumption of chocolate per year is in ———.

   a. France
   b. Switzerland

Answers: 1. b; 2. a; 3. a; 4. b; 5. a; 6. b; 7. b; 8. b

2. Look at the examples of different tastes. Try to add more examples for e

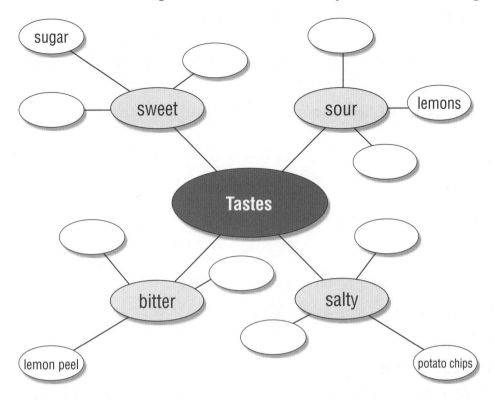

3. Now number the tastes in order of your preference (1 = like most, 4 = like least, etc.). Then compare your preferences in groups.

2 LISTENING PRACTICE

A Focus on the Listening Skill: Predicting

> **LISTENING SKILL**
>
> Before you listen to a talk or lecture, try to predict what it might be about. Look at the title and/or any included photos and think about (a) what you know about the topic and (b) what someone might say or write about it. Even if your predictions are not correct, just thinking about ideas before you start can help you understand a text more easily.

1. Work with a partner. Look at the title of a lecture. Discuss what you think the lecture might be about. Then answer the questions that follow.

Sweet and Sour:
The Science of Taste and Why We Like What We Like

ou think different people like different foods?

the same foods now that you liked as a child? If not, how has your taste

our taste in food is something we inherit from our families, something
our culture, or both? Explain.

of topics. Check the ones you think might be discussed in the

_____ 1. Babies and taste

_____ 2. Food cravings

_____ 3. Nutrition in different countries

_____ 4. Food preferences in different countries

_____ 5. Why some people don't eat breakfast

_____ 6. Why some people like bitter-tasting food

B Listening for Main Ideas

Listen to the lecture about food tastes. Note which topics from exercise 2 above
are discussed in the lecture.

C Listening for More Detail

Listen to the lecture again. Choose the correct answer to complete each
statement. Then compare answers with a partner. Listen again if necessary.

1. According to the "wisdom of the body" theory, we want certain food because _____.
   a. we need the nutrients
   b. we like the taste
   c. we need the nutrients and we like the taste

2. The "wisdom of the body" theory doesn't fully explain our eating habits, because _____.
   a. different people like different foods
   b. people have different ideas about nutrition
   c. we often eat food low in nutrition and don't like food high in nutrition

3. Babies prefer sweet drinks _____.
   a. about three days after they are born
   b. on the day they are born
   c. on their first birthday

4. Babies don't mind the pain of an injection as much if _____.
   a. they have something to eat before the shot
   b. they have some sugar before the shot
   c. they have some sugar after the shot

5. According to a recent study, children aged five to nine years old _____.
   a. like the flavor of citric acid
   b. can't taste citric acid
   c. dislike the flavor of citric acid

6. _____ don't usually like bitter flavors.
   a. Children
   b. Pregnant women
   c. Children and pregnant women

7. A study showed that if a woman drank carrot juice when she was pregnant, her baby _____.
   a. wouldn't like carrot-flavored cereal
   b. would like carrot-flavored cereal more than other babies
   c. would like carrot-flavored cereal as much as other babies

8. A study on cravings found that _____.
   a. women everywhere crave chocolate
   b. men and women in Egypt crave chocolate
   c. there are cultural differences in who craves chocolate

D Thinking and Speaking

Discuss these questions in pairs or in small groups.

1. Which piece of information in the lecture was most surprising to you?

2. Do you have any examples from your own experience that support the theories mentioned in the lecture? If so, explain them.

3. What are some foods that people typically crave in your culture?

4. Do you think food research is helpful? If so, in what ways is it helpful?

3 VOCABULARY: Verbs + -ing Form or Infinitive

Use verbs such as *like, love,* and *hate* to talk about preferences. Some of these verbs are followed by the infinitive form of a verb, some are followed by the *-ing* form of a verb, and some can be followed by either form.

🎧 1. Listen to the conversation between two friends. What are they discussing?

🎧 2. Listen again. Which verbs from the following chart do the speakers use?

Verb Followed by -ing	Verb Followed by Infinitive (to)	Verb Followed by -ing or Infinitive
don't mind	would like	like
can't stand	would love	love
enjoy	would prefer	prefer
dislike	want	hate
don't feel like	refuse	

3. For each item below, circle the *-ing* form, the infinitive, or both.

1. Scientists want (learning/to learn) more about what people eat.

2. He loves (having/to have) breakfast first thing in the morning.

3. Babies don't mind (getting/to get) an injection as much if they have something sweet beforehand.

4. A study found that babies enjoyed (eating/to eat) carrot-flavored cereal more if their mothers drank carrot juice during pregnancy.

5. A lot of children refuse (eating/to eat) nutritious foods.

6. Some people hate (eating/to eat) sweets.

4. Answer the questions. Then compare answers with a partner.

1. Is there anything that you refuse to eat?

2. What seasonings do you like to put on your food?

3. What are the ingredients in a dish that you love eating or making?

4. Do you prefer to eat certain foods at certain times of the year?

4 LISTENING PRACTICE

A Preparing to Listen

1. Look at these statistics about food and eating habits in the United States. Try to complete them by using the figures in the box. (The answers are at the end of the exercise.)

$2,030 $136 million   4.2 $2,780

1. The number of meals that the average person eats out each week is _____.

2. The average annual household expenditure for food away from home is _____.

3. The average annual household expenditure for food at home is _____.

4. The amount to be spent every day at 4:00 P.M. on dinner _____.

Source: *Kiplinger's Personal Finance Magazine,* October 2000

Answers: 1. 4.2; 2. $2,780; 3. $2,030; 4. $136 million

2. You're going to listen to an interview with a food scientist about changes in eating habits. Work with a partner and talk about what you know about the topic and what you think the scientist might say. Discuss how you think eating habits in the United States have changed in the last 10–20 years.

B Listening for Main Ideas

Listen to the interview with a food scientist. Check each of the topics that are discussed in the interview.

_____ 1. Eating out and eating at home

_____ 2. Amount of vegetables eaten

_____ 3. Consumption of soft drinks and milk

_____ 4. Variety of foods

_____ 5. Types of supermarkets

_____ 6. Quality and quantity of food

C Listening for More Detail

Write down some notes about what was said about each of the following topics. Then listen to the radio interview again and add more details.

1. The biggest change in eating habits _____

_____

2. Changes in drinking soft drinks and milk _____

_____

3. The effects of income on diet _____

_____

4. Prediction for the future _____

_____

5. The effect of immigration _____

_____

6. Surprising trends _____

_____

D Thinking and Speaking

1. Work with a partner. Think of as many answers as you can for the following questions:

    1. How do you think eating habits will change in the next ten years?

    2. How do you think eating habits should change in the next ten years?

2. Compare and discuss your lists in groups.

5 PRONUNCIATION: Intonation with Questions

FYI Intonation is the way your voice goes up and down when you speak. *Wh-*questions (questions that use *Who, What, When, Where, Why,* and *How*) and *Yes/No* questions have different intonation patterns.

1. Listen to these questions from the radio interview, and identify them as *Wh-*questions (*Wh*) or *Yes/No* questions (*Y/N*).

    _____ 1. So, what's one of the biggest changes in eating habits that you've found?

    _____ 2. Does your research suggest that this trend will continue?

    _____ 3. What else does your research predict for the future?

    _____ 4. Were there any surprises in your predictions?

2. Which type of question has rising (↗) intonation at the end? Which type of question has falling (↘) intonation at the end?

    _____ 1. *Wh-* questions
          a. rising intonation at the end
          b. falling intonation at the end

    _____ 2. *Yes/No* questions
          a. rising intonation at the end
          b. falling intonation at the end

3. Practice asking the questions with appropriate intonation. Then listen again and check your intonation.

6 SPEAKING SKILLS: Hesitating and Taking Time to Think

SPEAKING SKILL

It's OK to pause and take time to think when speaking. You can use the expressions below to avoid silence and give yourself time to think.

Hmm	That's a good question	Let me think
Well	Let's see	It depends

1. Listen to someone being interviewed about eating habits. What two changes in eating are mentioned?

2. Listen again. Which expressions do the speakers use?

7 SPEAKING PRACTICE

1. Work with a partner. Read the questionnaire. Then add at least three more questions about food and eating.

Food and Eating Questionnaire

1. What is one way your eating habits have changed in the past year?

_____

2. What is the most unusual thing you have eaten?

_____

3. Is there one food that you eat every day? If so, what?

_____

4. Do you prefer eating out or eating at home?

_____

2. Change partners and take turns asking and answering the questions. Use expressions from section 6 if you need to pause and take time to think while speaking. Make notes of your partner's answers.

3. Work in groups and compare your answers. How similar or different are they? Try to summarize some of your findings with phrases such as *most of us*, *some of us*, *only a few of us*, and *none of us*.

8 | TAKING SKILLS FURTHER

Try to practice predicting when you're watching or listening to the news, listening to a radio program, or reading a newspaper. Before you start, think about the topic and what you already know about it. Talk about your experiences in the next class.

 For additional listening practice on the topic of food, go to the *Open Forum* Web site (www.oup.com/elt/openforum) and follow the links.

CHAPTER 4 Visual Art

ABOUT THIS CHAPTER

Topic:	Visual art
Listening Texts:	Radio interview about Aboriginal art; lecture in an art museum
Listening Skill Focus:	Listening for main points
Speaking Skill Focus:	Using imprecision
Vocabulary:	Words and expressions related to art
Pronunciation:	The schwa sound

1 INTRODUCING THE TOPIC

Work in small groups. Look at the pictures and discuss the questions.

1. Do you enjoy looking at art?
2. What artists can you name?
3. Do you have a favorite artist?
4. What type of art do you like best?
5. Do you draw, paint, or make any kind of art? If not, do you know anyone who does?
6. Where—apart from museums—do you usually see examples of visual art (paintings, photography, sculpture, etc.)?

A Preparing to Listen

1. Work with a partner. Look at the photographs and discuss who you think the people are, where they are, and what they are doing.

2. These words are often used when talking about the visual arts. Match each word to its definition. Use a dictionary if necessary.

   __d__ 1. image   a. the way something is made or a painting is done

   _____ 2. symbol   b. a person in a painting or photograph

   _____ 3. figure   c. an image that represents or stands for something else

   _____ 4. abstract   d. a picture or description of something

   _____ 5. style   e. not realistic or lifelike

B Focus on the Listening Skill: Listening for Main Points

> **LISTENING SKILL**
>
> The first time you listen to a recording, do not try to listen for every detail. Instead, concentrate on the main points. Main points are often repeated more than once, and/or followed by details and examples.

🎧 Listen to an interview about Australian Aboriginal art. As you listen, check the three main points that are made. (All of the points are mentioned.)

   _____ a. Aboriginal art has lasted a long time.

   _____ b. The Aboriginal people are the original native Australians.

   _____ c. Aboriginal art is about the "dream time."

   _____ d. Aboriginal people didn't have a written language.

   _____ e. The most important thing for the artists is doing the art, not keeping or selling it.

   _____ f. Some paintings sell for thousands of dollars.

C Listening for More Detail

Listen to the interview again. As you listen, choose the correct answer for each item. Then compare answers with a partner. Listen again if necessary.

1. One reason that Aboriginal art is so popular is that _____.
   a. it has lasted for thousands of years
   b. the artists live in remote areas
   c. it is done on rocks

2. Researchers know that the art is very old because _____.
   a. the Aboriginal people have had little contact with outsiders
   b. the same symbols and patterns have been found in ancient rock carvings
   c. the artists are all old people

3. The "dream time" refers to _____.
   a. night time
   b. an imaginary time in the future
   c. the beginning of the world

4. Older people do the art because _____.
   a. they have traveled more than younger people
   b. they have more free time
   c. they have memorized many stories

5. Which of these phrases best describes the kind of art that the Aboriginal people do?
   a. Landscape painting
   b. Abstract painting
   c. Portrait painting

6. For the artists, the art _____.
   a. is less important than the artistic process
   b. is primarily a way to make money
   c. is a way to communicate with their ancestors

7. Which is the most recent form of Aboriginal art?
   a. Body painting
   b. Paintings on the ground
   c. Paintings on canvas

8. What is one reason that the art has only recently become popular?
   a. Aboriginal culture was not appreciated.
   b. It was too expensive.
   c. The artists gave the paintings away.

D Thinking and Speaking

Work with a partner. Make a list of the ways that Aboriginal art is different from more conventional art (e.g., a painting by a famous artist that you might see in a museum). Then compare your list with another pair.

Aboriginal Art	Conventional Art
Artists are not trained.	Many artists study art.

3 VOCABULARY: Words and Expressions Related to Art

1. Read the descriptions. Then add the words in bold to the mind map.

Most Aboriginal painting is not **realistic**. It's done in an abstract style. There are many repeated **lines, dots, and circles**. It's **colorful,** often with deep, earthy colors. There are **shapes and symbols** that appear again and again. Often there is a snake, which may represent water, or a river, snaking through the desert. Other **figures** might represent animals or people.

This **landscape** was painted by the Flemish artist Pieter Brueghel the Younger. It shows a **traditional scene** in the countryside. **In the foreground** there are some harvesters eating, and there are many people working **in the center** of the picture. There's a lot of detail in the picture: the trees, birds, and houses are really clearly drawn, even **in the background**. The overall effect is **calm** and peaceful.

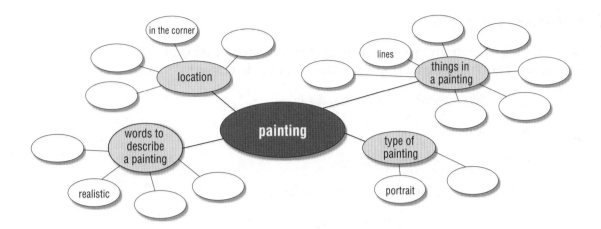

2. Work with a partner. Think of a painting or a photograph that you know well, for example, something that hangs on a wall in your home. Describe it, using some of the words from the mind map.

4 | LISTENING PRACTICE

A Preparing to Listen

1. Work with a partner. Look at the picture of *American Gothic,* a famous American painting. Describe the painting as clearly as you can.

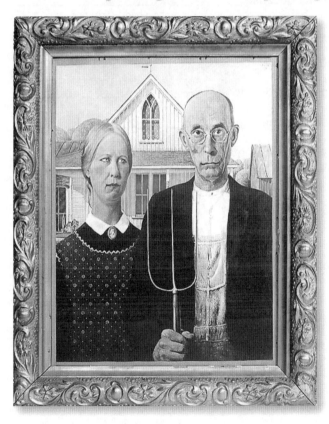

2. With your partner, discuss the people in the painting. Who do you think they are? Where do you think they are? What do you think their personalities are like?

B Listening for Main Ideas

Listen to a guide in an art museum talk about the painting *American Gothic*. As you listen, check the three main points that are discussed.

_____ a. U.S. history during Grant Wood's life

_____ b. The artist

_____ c. A description of the painting

_____ d. The process: how the painting was made

_____ e. People's reaction to the painting

C Listening for More Detail

1. These sentences form a summary of the talk. Read the sentences and fill in all the information that you can remember. Then listen to the talk again, and complete the summary as you listen. Compare answers with a partner.

   1. *American Gothic* is very well known because _____.

   2. It was painted by Grant Wood in (year) _____.

   3. The style of the painting is like folk art, but Wood was influenced by _____.

   4. The painting is called *American Gothic* because _____.

   5. The models for the painting were _____.

   6. The people are wearing clothes from (period) _____.

   7. Most people feel that the people in the picture look _____.

   8. Some people think that Grant Wood was making fun of _____.

2. Listen again to the part of the talk where the guide describes the painting in detail. As you listen, number the topics in the order they are mentioned. Then look at the picture with a partner and discuss what was said about each topic.

   _____ a. The background

   _____ b. Expressions on the faces

   _____ c. Gothic lines in the picture

   _____ d. The man's clothes

   _____ e. The pitchfork

   _____ f. The woman's dress

D Thinking and Speaking

Work in a group. Discuss the questions.

1. Many people think that *American Gothic* is ironic—in other words, that the picture seems to idealize country life, but also has a negative meaning. What does it mean to you?

2. What did you learn about the painting? How does knowing the background of a painting help you to appreciate it?

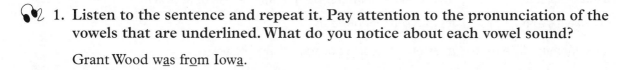

5 PRONUNCIATION: The Schwa Sound

🎧 1. Listen to the sentence and repeat it. Pay attention to the pronunciation of the vowels that are underlined. What do you notice about each vowel sound?

Grant Wood w<u>a</u>s fr<u>o</u>m Iow<u>a</u>.

> **FYI** The vowel sound in unstressed syllables sounds something like *uh*. It is called the schwa, and it is represented by the phonological symbol /ə/. The schwa is also used in weak forms like *a, the,* and *of.*

🎧 2. Listen to these words and repeat them, using the schwa sound. Vowels with the schwa sound are underlined.

<u>A</u>meric<u>a</u>n
s<u>u</u>pposed
prob<u>a</u>bly
phot<u>o</u>graph
fam<u>ou</u>s
wom<u>a</u>n

🎧 3. Listen to these sentences and fill in the missing words.

1. He _____ American painter.

2. His sister _____ model.

3. It's _____ photograph.

4. Who is _____ be?

5. It's _____ mystery.

4. Underline the schwa sounds in the sentences above. Then practice saying the sentences.

6 | SPEAKING SKILLS: Using Imprecision

> ### SPEAKING SKILL
>
> When you are not sure that you have chosen the right word, or you want to seem less direct, use expressions such as the ones in the chart below to express imprecision.

Expression	Example
about/approximately	*It's about ten o'clock.*
kind of/sort of	*It's a kind of sculpture. Her painting is sort of abstract.*
it's like/it's as if	*It's as if she's ignoring us.*
or something (like that)	*It tastes like peaches or something like that.*

1. Read the description of *American Gothic.* Then listen to what was actually said in the lecture. What are some of the ways that the spoken version is different from the written one? What is the effect?

   Although the style of the painting is like folk art, the people aren't idealized in any way. They look unfriendly. You get the feeling that you're not welcome. They're shutting you out. They're defending their world from outsiders.

2. Listen to a longer extract and fill in the missing words.

   For most people, the interesting thing about the picture is the expressions on the

   faces of the couple . . . because although the . . . style of the painting is like folk

   art (1) _or something like that_, the people aren't idealized in any way. They

   look (2) _____ unfriendly . . . you get the feeling that you're

   not welcome. They're (3) _____ shutting you out. . . .

   (4) _____ . . . they're defending their world from outsiders. The

   man looks as if he'd use that pitchfork as a weapon if necessary. . . . And the woman

   looks . . . (5) _____ suspicious. . . . (6) _____

   she's worrying about somebody stealing her laundry (7) _____.

1. Work with a partner. Partner A: Choose one of the photographs below to describe. Partner B: Close your book and listen to your partner's description. Can you imagine the photograph? Take turns describing each of the photographs in the same way. Try to use some of the expressions from section 6.

2. Imagine you are choosing these pictures for a book of photographs showing American life today. Which aspects of American life does each picture show? Choose the photo that you think would be the best one to include in the book.

8 | TAKING SKILLS FURTHER

Outside of class, listen to people describing things or ask a native speaker to describe a picture to you in detail. Listen for some of the expressions in section 6. How many do you hear? In the next class, discuss your findings.

For additional listening practice on the topic of art, go to the *Open Forum* Web site (www.oup.com/elt/openforum) and follow the links.

CHAPTER **5** Life Science

Topics:	Ocean research; condor preservation
Listening Texts:	Radio program on ocean research; informational talk at a ranger station
Listening Skill Focus:	Working out unknown vocabulary
Speaking Skill Focus:	Asking for further information
Vocabulary:	Adjective suffixes *-ful* and *-less*
Pronunciation:	Verb endings

1 INTRODUCING THE TOPIC

1. Work with a partner. Look at the pictures. What are the people doing? What are some possible reasons for doing work like this? What are some possible benefits?

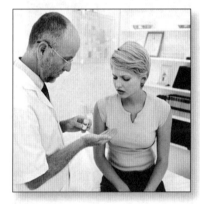 

2. Compare and discuss your answers in small groups.

2 LISTENING PRACTICE

A Preparing to Listen

1. Look at the list of words below. Write them in the chart in the category they are related to, either "Oceans" or "Medicine." Use a dictionary if necessary.

anatomy	bacteria	beach	crab
cancer	coral	fish	heart disease
human disease	painkiller	prescription drugs	sand
snail	whales		

Oceans	Medicine

2. Compare answers with a partner. What other words can you add to the two categories?

B Listening for Main Ideas

Listen to a radio program about research in oceans. Then match each creature to an area of research.

1. horseshoe crab

2. skatefish

3. toadfish

4. snail

5. coral

6. whale

_____ a. painkillers

_____ b. muscles/heart disease

_____ c. detergents

_____ d. contamination/sterilization

_____ e. eye disease

_____ f. cancer

C Listening for More Detail

Read the questions and answer the ones that you can. Then listen to the radio program again and answer the rest of the questions. Compare answers with a partner. Listen again if necessary.

1. What portion of prescription drugs come from natural sources? _____

2. How much of the Earth's surface is covered by water? _____

3. Why are scientists interested in the skate fish? _____

4. Why can scientists study more of the ocean nowadays than they could in the past?

   _____

5. When did scientists discover that the horseshoe crab could be useful in medicine?

   _____

6. What is special about the toadfish? _____

D Focus on the Listening Skill: Working Out Unknown Vocabulary

> **LISTENING SKILL**
>
> If you don't know what a word or expression means, pay attention to the words around it and the general meaning of the sentence. Also, use your background knowledge to help you. This can help you work out the meaning.

1. Read and listen to the extract from the radio program. Then look at item 1 below to see how the meaning of *ancient* was worked out. Choose the correct meaning for the word in item 2, and explain the reason for your choice.

   Now, you may not realize it, but there are already some medical substances in use today that were derived from the sea. The horseshoe crab, a very old—actually ancient—marine creature, is one of the most famous examples.

   1. *Ancient* probably means ____.
      a. very delicious
      (b.) extremely old

      How did you know? *Because of "very old" before it* .

   2. *Marine* probably means ____.
      a. of the sea
      b. a meat eater

      How did you know? _____ .

2. For each item, listen to the extract and try to work out the meaning of the word in italics. Then compare your answers with a partner and discuss the reasons for your choices.

1. *Contamination* probably means _____.
   a. medication
   b. something bad or harmful

2. *Blindness* probably means _____.
   a. not being able to see
   b. not being able to hear

3. *Failing* probably means _____.
   a. getting stronger or better
   b. getting weaker and not working well

4. *Combat* probably means _____.
   a. to work hard
   b. to fight against

5. *Stains* probably means _____.
   a. dirt or spots on clothing
   b. colors

E Thinking and Speaking

Discuss these questions in small groups.

1. What remedies do you know of that come from plants or animals?
2. What do you think are the most important problems or issues in medicine today?
3. What do you think are possible risks to oceans and the environment with this kind of research?

3 VOCABULARY: Adjective Suffixes *-ful* and *-less*

> **FYI**
> You can use the suffixes *-ful* and *-less* to make adjectives from some nouns. The suffix *-ful* often means "with" or "full of." The suffix *-less* often means "without." For example, the word *careful* means "full of care" and *careless* means "without care."

1. Read the extract from the radio program. Underline the adjectives with the suffix *-ful*.

So, there's a lot of variety in the research. Some scientists caution that this is all a very slow process and that we have to be careful. It could take years for any one thing to be tested and proven safe and useful. But many researchers are still excited and hopeful.

2. Complete the chart by making adjectives from the nouns. Notice which nouns take only one of the suffixes. Pay attention to spelling with *beauty*; you will have to change *y* to *i*.

Noun	Adjective with *-ful*	Adjective with *-less*
1. care	careful	careless
2. use		
3. beauty		X
4. hope		
5. harm		
6. price	X	
7. help		
8. wonder		X
9. thought		
10. pain		

3. Complete each sentence with the appropriate adjective from the chart above.

1. Don't be _____careless_____ when you drive. You could have an accident.

2. The operation was _____. I didn't feel a thing.

3. This is such a _____ tool. I use it all the time.

4. Scientists are _____ they will find new medicines in nature.

5. I'm sorry, I wasn't thinking. It was _____ of me not to offer

   to help.

6. It was the best party I've ever been to. It was _____!

7. This antique necklace is _____. No amount of money could

   ever replace it.

8. The researchers were disappointed when they found that the new substance was

   _____ against disease.

A Preparing to Listen

1. Look at the photo of a California condor. What do you know about condors? What can you guess from the photo? What other large birds do you know of?

2. Read the condor facts below. Try to complete them by using the numbers in the box. (Answers are at the bottom of the page.)

> 9   55   100   15,000

Condor Facts

1. A condor's wingspan can be more than ____ feet.
2. Adult condors have bare, pink heads. The color gets more intense when they are excited.
3. Condors can fly as fast as ____ MPH.
4. Condors can fly as high as ____ feet.
5. Condors were near extinction in 1987. Now there are almost ____ living in the wild.

B Listening for Main Ideas

Listen to a biologist talk about a program to save condors and reintroduce them into the wild. Number the topics in the order they are mentioned.

____ a. Use of global positioning system (GPS)

____ b. Working together and socializing

____ c. Background and history

____ d. Raising baby condors

1. 9; 3. 55; 4. 15,000; 5. 100

C Listening for More Detail

Read the questions and answer the ones you can. Then listen to the lecture again and complete your answers. Compare answers with a partner. Listen again if necessary.

1. When did the U.S. Fish & Wildlife Service start their breeding program?
2. What are the three regions mentioned where wild condors live now?
3. What are two points mentioned that make it difficult to attach the GPS units to condors?
4. What is one thing biologists have learned as a result of using GPS?
5. What didn't the baby condors learn in the early days of the program?
6. What are the humans raising baby condors trained to do now?
7. How do condors learn how to find food?
8. What example does the speaker give to show that condors like to socialize?

D Working Out Unknown Vocabulary

For each item, listen to the extract and try to work out the meaning of the word in italics. Then compare answers with a partner and discuss the reasons for your choices.

1. *Offspring* probably means _____.
   a. parents
   b. babies

2. *Puppet* probably means _____.
   a. a picture of a person or animal
   b. a model of a person or animal that you put on your hand and move with your fingers

3. *Harassing* probably means _____.
   a. annoying or putting pressure on regularly
   b. feeding

4. *Scavengers* probably means _____.
   a. animals that hunt live animals for food
   b. animals that finds dead animals to eat

5 PRONUNCIATION: Verb Endings

It can be difficult to hear verb endings because they are not usually stressed. But if you pay attention to them, verb endings give you information about time and tense. This can help you understand a whole sentence better.

1. Listen to each item and circle the letter of the sentence you hear.

   1. a. They monitor the condors.
      b. They're monitoring the condors.

   2. a. The GPS unit gives us data.
      b. The GPS units give us data.

   3. a. They learn a lot about condors.
      b. They've learned a lot about condors.

2. Listen to each item and circle the verb form you hear.

   1. learn/learned

   2. knock/knocking

   3. harass/harassing

   4. teach/teaches

   5. raise/raising

   6. socialize/socializing

3. Choose one sentence from each pair in exercise 1 above, or make your own. Read the sentences aloud to a partner. See if your partner can identify the correct sentence and verb ending.

6 | SPEAKING SKILLS: Asking for Further Information

SPEAKING SKILL

Don't be afraid to ask for clarification or further information in a conversation if you need to. The questions below may help you clarify something you've heard.

> How many/Where/When/What did you say . . . ?
> Can/Could you repeat that?
> Can/Could you explain . . . ?
> Can/Could you give another example of . . . ?
> What does (X) mean?
> What did you mean . . . ?
> What did you say about . . . ?

1. Listen to the questions people asked the biologist after his talk about condors. What did they ask about?

2. Listen again. Which questions from above did the people use? What other questions could you ask?

7 | SPEAKING PRACTICE

1. Imagine you are on a committee that will give $25,000 to research programs. The money must be divided between two or more programs. Read the information below, and decide which programs you think should receive the money.

Program A
> A research study on bird migration. Scientists believe that information on migration could offer useful and important information on weather patterns and climate change.

Program B
> A study of traditional remedies used to combat common illnesses in different countries. Researchers believe that they could gain new information and ideas to produce affordable medicines for large groups of people.

Program C
> A plan to establish a marine reserve to protect fish, plants, and coral in the ocean. Scientists believe that without protection, many sea creatures are in danger of extinction.

Program D
> A program to search for possible new medicines in rainforests around the world. This program will also include research into ways to protect rainforests.

---

2. Work in small groups. Take turns presenting your plan to divide up the money. Give reasons for your choices. When you're listening to other plans, try to use expressions from section 6 to ask for clarification and further information.

8 | TAKING SKILLS FURTHER

Outside of class, pay attention to unknown words or expressions you hear. Try to use the contexts, your background knowledge, and/or any other clues to work out the meanings. In the next class, give an example of a word or expression that you worked out the meaning for and explain how you did it.

For additional listening practice on the topic of life science, go to the *Open Forum* Web site (www.oup.com/elt/openforum) and follow the links.

Topic:	Work
Listening Texts:	Lecture about European and U.S. work habits; radio program about freelancing
Listening Skill Focus:	Identifying organizing phrases
Speaking Skill Focus:	Expressing opinions
Vocabulary:	Words and expressions related to work
Pronunciation:	Contractions with *be* and *have*

1 INTRODUCING THE TOPIC

Look at the statistics and answer the questions below. Then compare answers with a partner.

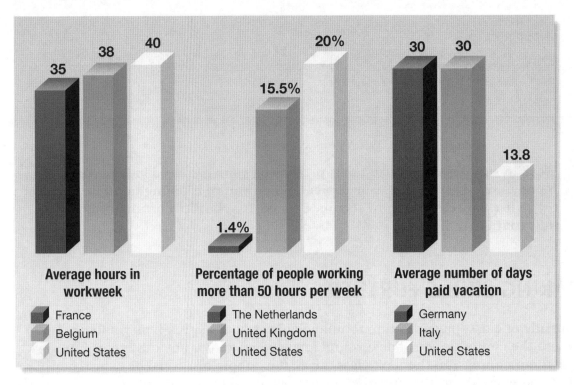

Average hours in workweek
- France
- Belgium
- United States

Percentage of people working more than 50 hours per week
- The Netherlands
- United Kingdom
- United States

Average number of days paid vacation
- Germany
- Italy
- United States

1. Which country on the list has the shortest workweek?

2. In which country do the most people work more than 50 hours a week?

3. How does the United States compare to Germany and Italy in the amount of vacation time that workers receive?

4. What generalization can you make about work habits in Europe and the United States?

2 LISTENING PRACTICE

A Preparing to Listen

You are going to hear a lecture about the reasons for the difference between European and U.S. working hours. Work in small groups. Look at the list of possible reasons, and discuss which reasons you think are most likely.

_____ a. U.S. companies introduced the two-week vacation.

_____ b. Most European countries have laws about vacation time.

_____ c. U.S. workers earn more than Europeans do.

_____ d. The U.S. workplace is more competitive.

_____ e. Many more Europeans than Americans are unemployed.

B Listening for Main Ideas

Listen to the lecture. As you listen, check on the list above the two reasons the speaker gives for the differences in working habits between Europe and the United States.

C Listening for More Detail

Listen to the lecture again. As you listen, write *T* for true or *F* for false for each item. Then compare answers with a partner. Listen again if necessary.

_____ 1. The difference in work habits between the United States and Europe is getting smaller.

_____ 2. Americans introduced both the 2-week vacation and the 40-hour workweek.

_____ 3. In the past, Americans had more leisure time than Europeans did.

_____ 4. Americans have more laws about leisure time.

_____ 5. Workers in Britain work longer hours than workers in other European countries.

_____ 6. All employees in the United States receive two weeks' paid vacation.

_____ 7. Some workers in the United States do not use the vacation time that they have.

_____ 8. American workers have more job security.

D Focus on the Listening Skill: Identifying Organizing Phrases

> **LISTENING SKILL**
>
> In formal talks or lectures, speakers often use organizing phrases to announce what they are going to say or do, to signal a change in topic, or to summarize the information that has been presented. Verbs like *look at, describe, point out,* or *compare* are often used in these phrases. Listen for these phrases to understand the structure of the lecture better.

1. Listen to the lecture again. As you listen, number the organizing phrases in the order you hear them.

   _____ a. Compare that to

   _____ b. I'd like to point out that

   _____ c. I'd like to talk about

   _____ d. I'm going to suggest

   _____ e. I've described

   _____ f. Let's turn to

   _____ g. Now if you look at

   _____ h. We're going to look at

2. Look at the organizing phrases above and decide what the function of each phrase is. Then add the phrases to the list below. Can you add any more phrases?

   Announcing what the speaker is going to say or do

   I'd like to point out that

   _____

   _____

   _____

   Signaling a change in topic

   Compare that to

   _____

   _____

   Summarizing

   _____

E Thinking and Speaking

1. Look at the chart. Company A offers four weeks of paid vacation time. Company B offers only one week. Complete the chart on your own.

Which company do you think has . . .	Company A	Company B
1. more productivity?		
2. better motivated employees?		
3. higher salaries?		
4. less stress?		
5. greater job satisfaction?		

2. Compare your answers in small groups. Which system do you think is better for the employer, and why?

3 VOCABULARY: Words and Expressions Related to Work

1. Read the text. Pay attention to the words in bold. Then write the correct word next to each definition below.

More and more workers today are **self-employed**. Rather than work for one **employer** and getting a regular **salary**, they find their own work and organize their own schedules. Many of these are **freelancers** who may work for several different employers. Some people work **part-time**, say 20 hours a week. Or maybe they work full-time, but they are **temporary**: an employer **hires** them for a specific **project** for a specific period of time. Many workers say that this gives them more flexibility to organize their lives. They can take **time off** when they want to. But of course they don't get any **benefits** like health insurance or paid vacations. They also have less **job security**. They are more likely to **get laid off** if the economic climate is bad.

1. working for yourself: _____self-employed_____

2. free time: _____

3. money that employees are paid on a regular basis: _____

4. someone who pays people to work for them: _____

5. the opposite of full-time: _____

6. for a short time, not permanent: _____

7. gives someone a job: _____

8. to lose your job, often because there isn't enough work: _____

9. a job or a specific task: _____

10. self-employed people (often writers or artists) who work for one or more

employers: _____

11. the feeling that you are likely to keep your job; that you aren't likely to be fired or laid off: _____

12. extra services or payments given to an employee in addition to his or her salary:

_____

2. **Complete the sentences with the words in bold from the paragraph in exercise 1. You may have to change the form of some of the words.**

1. I make a lot of money; I have a high _salary_____.

2. The job comes with excellent _____: health insurance and four weeks of paid vacation.

3. After this project is finished, I'm going to take some _____ to be with my family.

4. The boss interviewed me and gave me the job. She _____ me.

5. The receptionist is out sick, so we've hired a _____ worker until Friday.

6. I'm not worried about losing my job. I have plenty of _____.

7. My sister designs web pages for many different clients. She's a

_____.

8. If the economic situation gets any worse, some workers will lose their jobs. They'll

_____.

3. **Work with a partner. Describe the kind of job that you would like to have. Use as many of the words as you can.**

Example: *I'd like to be **hired** by a high-tech company. I'd like to get a high **salary**, and . . .*

A Preparing to Listen

You are going to listen to a radio program about self-employment in the United States. Think of some advantages and disadvantages of being self-employed, and add them to the lists below. Then compare your lists in small groups.

Advantages of self-employment	*Disadvantages of self-employment*
You can be your own boss	Long hours

B Listening for Main Ideas

Listen to an extract from a radio program about self-employment. As you listen, note your answers to the following questions.

1. How many jobs does the man have?

2. What does the woman do?

3. Check the three aspects of self-employment that Jenny Huang discusses.

_____ a. Some problems of self-employment

_____ b. Financial aspects of self-employment

_____ c. The kind of people who are self-employed

_____ d. Why self-employment is a growing trend

C Listening for More Detail

Read the questions and answer the ones you can. Then listen to the interview again and note your answers as you listen. Compare answers with a partner. Listen again if necessary.

1. Why does the man like being a substitute teacher?

2. Who pays for his health benefits?

3. Why did the woman decide to start her own business?

4. Why doesn't she have many expenses?

5. What would she like to do in the future?

6. What kind of work do self-employed people often do?

7. What three reasons does Jenny Huang give for the rise in self-employment?

8. According to Jenny Huang, what do self-employed people have to be good at?

D Working Out Unknown Vocabulary

Listen to the extracts from the interview. Listen for the words and expressions in italics. Choose the correct meaning for each word or expression.

1. *On the front lines* probably means _____.
   a. standing in line
   b. directly experiencing a situation

2. *Juggle* probably means _____.
   a. deal with different activities at the same time
   b. travel from place to place

3. *Go out on my own* probably means _____.
   a. leave my job
   b. start my own business

4. *Getting by* probably means _____.
   a. becoming very successful
   b. managing with the money that is available

5. *Entrepreneurs* probably are _____.
   a. people who have their own businesses
   b. people who work alone

E Thinking and Speaking

Discuss the questions in small groups.

1. Look back to the lists of advantages and disadvantages that you made in section A. Which ones were mentioned in the interviews? Can you add any more to the lists, based on what you heard in the program?

2. Which would you prefer: to be self-employed or to have a steady job with one employer?

3. If you were to start your own business, what kind of business would it be?

5 | PRONUNCIATION: Contractions with *Be* and *Have*

FYI Forms of the auxiliary verbs *be* and *have* are often contracted. For example, *it is* and *it has* are both contracted to *it's*, and *they are* becomes *they're*. Contractions can be difficult to hear.

1. Listen to the extracts. As you listen, fill in the missing contractions. Then compare answers with a partner.

   Extract 1

   Well, I don't have very many expenses because (1) _____I'm_____ living and

   working at my parents' house, so I don't pay rent. (2) _____ going

   OK. (3) _____ getting by. It takes a while, you know, to get known.

   (4) _____ been a learning experience. (5) _____ learned a lot

   about managing a business.

   Extract 2

   Well, some of (6) _____ economic. There are people (7) _____ been laid

   off, so (8) _____ decided to go out on their own. Another reason is the growth

   of the software industry and the media, where (9) _____ always used a lot of

   freelancers: writers and programmers and so on. There are a lot of people working in

   those areas now. But (10) _____ also been a change in attitudes.

2. Write three sentences about work that you have done or work that you would like to do. Include five different contractions in your sentences. Read your sentences to a partner. Then check your answers.

6 SPEAKING SKILLS: Expressing Opinions

SPEAKING SKILL

When you are giving opinions in a discussion, use the expressions in the chart below to respond to the other person's opinion and introduce your own.

Giving an Opinion	Agreeing	Agreeing in Part	Disagreeing
I think . . .	Yes/Yeah.	Yes/Yeah, but . . .	I don't know. I think . . .
I don't think . . .	I agree.	Maybe, but . . .	I'm not sure about that.
	I know.	I guess so, but . . .	
	Absolutely.	I realize that, but . . .	

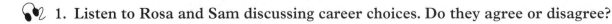 1. Listen to Rosa and Sam discussing career choices. Do they agree or disagree?

2. Listen again. Which expressions do you hear?

3. Try to re-create the conversation with a partner. Use the expressions from the chart.

7 SPEAKING PRACTICE

1. Work in pairs. Read the letters to an advice columnist. Choose one of the situations, and discuss what you think the person should do and why. Make notes. As you speak, try to use some of the phrases from section 6.

JOBWEEK

LETTERS TO THE EDITOR

I work as an accountant at a tax-preparation service in the small town where I grew up. My boss is an old friend of the family. He's a very nice man, but he's not very efficient. I've been working here for six years now, and the customers have started asking for me because they say I'm faster and more accurate.

Several of my clients have suggested that I open my own tax-preparation business, which would be a great opportunity for me. However, I feel bad about going into direct competition with my employer. What should I do?

–Laura

I'm thirty years old, and a single father with two young children. After several years of struggling as a freelance photographer, I recently got a job with the city. It's very stable, with good pay and full benefits for my kids.

The problem is, the job is incredibly boring. I don't feel like I'm learning anything. I find myself taking sick days that I don't really need, just to do something creative. I miss doing photography, which I really enjoyed even though it didn't pay very well. On the other hand, we need the regular salary and the benefits. Do I have to sell my soul to this job?

–Dan

2. Work with another pair that chose the same situation. Compare your opinions. Say if you agree or disagree.

3. Compare your suggestions as a class. How many different suggestions were given for each situation?

8 | TAKING SKILLS FURTHER

Outside of class, listen to a lecture or a formal talk about any topic. Note the organizing phrases that you hear. In the next class, compare your lists.

For additional listening practice on the topic of social studies, go to the *Open Forum* Web site (www.oup.com/elt/openforum) and follow the links.

Topics:	Different languages in the United States; endangered languages
Listening Texts:	Lecture about other languages in the United States; student presentation
Listening Skill Focus:	Intensive listening for numbers
Speaking Skill Focus:	Preparing for presentations
Vocabulary:	Expressions for approximations with numbers
Pronunciation:	Stress in numbers with -*ty* and -*teen*

1 | INTRODUCING THE TOPIC

1. Work with a partner. Try to answer the questions in the quiz. (Answers are at the bottom of the page.)

Language Quiz

1. **How many languages are spoken in the world today?**
   a. About 600
   b. About 6,000 to 8,000
   c. About 60,000

2. **How many different languages do people speak in the United States?**
   a. More than 30
   b. More than 300
   c. 30,000

3. **After English, what is the most widely spoken language in the United States?**
   a. Chinese
   b. Korean
   c. Spanish

4. **In which state is Chinese spoken by the most people?**
   a. California
   b. New York
   c. Texas

2. Check your answers to the quiz. Which fact surprises you most?

Answers: 1. b; 2. b; 3. c; 4. a

A Preparing to Listen

Look at the pie chart and text. Work in small groups and discuss the questions.

1. What percentage of people speak English at home?
2. What percentage of people speak another language?
3. Which four languages have the same percentage of speakers?
4. What languages do you think might come under "Other"?
5. Does any of this information surprise you?

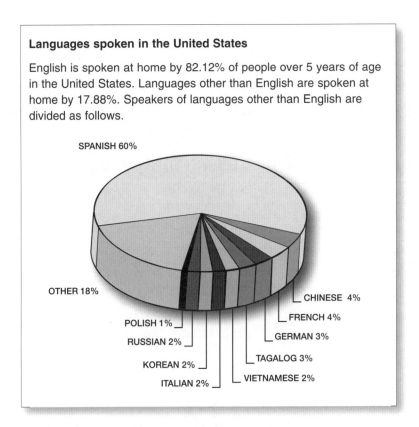

Languages spoken in the United States

English is spoken at home by 82.12% of people over 5 years of age in the United States. Languages other than English are spoken at home by 17.88%. Speakers of languages other than English are divided as follows.

B Listening for Main Ideas

 Listen to a lecture. Then choose the best summary.

The lecture is about _____.

a. the number of different languages used in the United States
b. data about language use in the United States and how it might be used
c. why it's important to look at language use in the United States

C Listening for More Detail

Listen to the lecture again, and answer the questions.

1. How many languages does the Modern Language Association focus on?

2. Where did the data come from?

3. Put these languages in order from the most common to the least common in the United States (1 = most common, 4 = least common):

    _____ a. Spanish

    _____ b. French

    _____ c. English

    _____ d. Chinese

4. How many people speak Korean in the United States?

5. In what two areas do the majority of Korean speakers live?

6. Are more languages spoken in Texas or New York?

D Focus on the Listening Skill: Intensive Listening for Numbers

> **LISTENING SKILL**
>
> It can be very important to hear numbers accurately in a lecture. However, numbers can be difficult to hear. Practice listening for numbers as much as possible.

1. Listen to the extract from the lecture. Fill in the blanks with the correct numbers. Then compare answers with a partner. Listen again if necessary.

In Texas, English is spoken at home by just over (1) _____68_____ percent of people.

Of the people who speak another language, (2) _____ percent speak Spanish,

and it's only (3) _____ or _____ percent for any of the other languages.

So Spanish really is the predominant language other than English in Texas. Now, you

can then compare that information to other states. For example, looking at the state

of New York . . . in New York, a little over (4) _____ percent of people speak

English at home. Of the speakers of other languages, (5) _____ percent speak

Spanish and then (6) _____ percent speak Chinese, (7) _____ percent

speak Italian, and (8) _____ percent speak Russian, and (9) _____

percent speak French.

E Thinking and Speaking

Discuss the questions with a partner. Then compare and discuss answers as a class.

1. Summarize the ways mentioned that the data could be important or useful. Can you add any other ideas?

2. The data showed that all the languages (other than English) are spoken more by older people than by children. Is this significant? Why or why not?

3 VOCABULARY: Expressions for Approximations with Numbers

1. These sentences from the lecture all have approximations in them. An approximation is a way to indicate that a number is not exact. For example, *about 900,000* means "not exactly 900,000." Look at the example and underline the other expressions used for approximation.

   1. There are <u>about</u> 900,000 Korean speakers in the United States.

   2. In Texas, English is spoken at home by just over 68 percent of people.

   3. In New York, a little over 72 percent of people speak English at home.

2. Look at the list of approximations. Complete the chart by categorizing them according to meanings.

   ~~about~~   a little over   ~~a little under~~   almost   around
   ~~just over~~   just under   less than   more than   something like

Approximately	More	Less
about	just over	a little under

3. Listen to the sentences and fill in the blanks with approximations from the chart above. Then compare answers with a partner. Listen again if necessary.

   1. In Michigan, _____ 92 percent of people speak English at home.

   2. _____ 72 percent of people speak English at home in New York.

   3. A language other than English is spoken by _____ 40 percent of people in California.

   4. There are _____ 100 students at the school right now.

   5. Many people believe that _____ half of all languages in the world could be lost.

   6. There are _____ 91,000 speakers of Chinese in Texas.

4. Use these ideas (or some of your own) to make three to five sentences containing numbers and approximations. Then read your sentences to a partner. See if your partner can hear the numbers and the approximations.

- the number of students that attend your school
- the population of your city
- the number of miles to a nearby city
- the age of a famous person
- the temperature outside

4 LISTENING PRACTICE

A Preparing to Listen

1. Read the information from a Web site about languages. What are the official languages of Canada? What are some examples of minority languages in Canada?

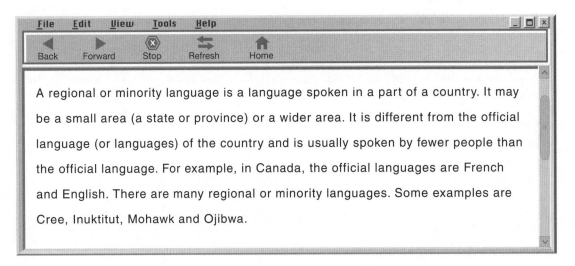

File   Edit   View   Tools   Help

Back   Forward   Stop   Refresh   Home

A regional or minority language is a language spoken in a part of a country. It may be a small area (a state or province) or a wider area. It is different from the official language (or languages) of the country and is usually spoken by fewer people than the official language. For example, in Canada, the official languages are French and English. There are many regional or minority languages. Some examples are Cree, Inuktitut, Mohawk and Ojibwa.

2. Try to match the regional or minority language to the country where it is spoken. (Answers are at the bottom of the page.)

Language	Country
_____ 1. Welsh	a. France
_____ 2. Provençal	b. Belgium
_____ 3. Mati Ke	c. United States
_____ 4. Walloon	d. Australia
_____ 5. Navajo	e. Wales

Answers: 1. e; 2. a; 3. d; 4. b; 5. c

3. Discuss the questions in pairs or small groups.

   1. Do you know of any other minority or regional languages?

   2. What are some of the issues related to these kinds of languages?

B Listening for Main Ideas

Listen to two students give a presentation in class. Number the topics in the order they are mentioned.

_____ Programs for reviving Native American languages

_____ Different opinions on how many languages exist today

_____ The situation with the Welsh language

_____ Criteria for deciding if a language is in danger

_____ Why the topic of language loss is important

C Listening for More Detail

Listen to the presentation again. Write down some notes about each of the items below. Then compare and discuss answers with a partner. Listen again if necessary.

1. Between 6,000 and 6,800	An estimate of number of languages in use in world
2. Half the world's languages	
3. 46 different people	
4. Different criteria	
5. Why preserve languages?	
6. The Welsh language	
7. 250 languages and 150 languages	
8. Ways to preserve Native American languages	

D Thinking and Speaking

Work with a partner. Summarize the different ideas or approaches mentioned for preserving languages. Then answer the questions.

   1. Which ideas do you think are most effective? Give reasons for your answers.

   2. Can you think of any other ideas? Have you heard of any other ideas?

   3. Do you think it's important to preserve dying languages? Why or why not?

5 PRONUNCIATION: Stress in Numbers with -ty and -teen

> Hearing the difference between numbers that end with -ty and numbers that end with -teen (for example, *fifty* and *fifteen*) can be difficult. It is often easier to hear the difference when the number is at the end of the sentence, but it can be harder when the number comes before a noun.

1. Listen to the sentences. Notice where the stress falls on the numbers. How is item 4 different from the others?

   1. There are fifty different languages.

   2. There are fifty.

   3. There are fifteen different languages.

   4. There are fifteen.

2. Listen to the sentences again. Is it easier to hear the difference between items 1 and 3, or items 2 and 4?

3. Listen to the sentences. For each one, choose the number that you hear. Compare answers with a partner. Listen again if necessary.

   1. My French book cost (sixty/sixteen) dollars.

   2. I have about (forty/fourteen) CDs.

   3. (Thirty/Thirteen) thousand people went to the concert.

   4. (Seventy/Seventeen) people work in my office.

   5. It was (eighty/eighteen) degrees Fahrenheit outside yesterday.

   6. (Fifty/Fifteen) million people watched that TV program last night.

4. Work with a partner. Take turns reading the sentences in exercise 3. Choose one of the possible numbers in each case. See if your partner can hear the correct number.

6 SPEAKING SKILLS: Preparing for Presentations

SPEAKING SKILL

> It is important to plan and prepare well for presentations. This will make your presentation better, and also help you feel more confident and relaxed when you present. On the next page you will look at some typical steps that people follow to prepare presentations.

1. Discuss these questions with a partner.

   1. How do you feel about public speaking, for example, giving a presentation to other students?

   2. How do you prepare for presentations?

2. Here are some steps that many people follow when preparing for a presentation. Put them in logical order. Compare answers with a partner.

   _____ **Select ideas:** Read over the ideas that you brainstormed. Take out ideas that do not work or are not relevant.

   _____ **Rehearse:** Practice in front of friends.

   __1__ **Brainstorm ideas:** Write down as many ideas as you can.

   _____ **Fill out an outline:** Add examples, details, statistics, etc., to explain and support your main points.

   _____ **Order ideas and outline:** Put the ideas in a logical order, and plan an outline of the main points in your presentation.

7 | SPEAKING PRACTICE

1. Choose one of the following topics about language (or use your own), and prepare a short presentation. Use the steps for preparing in exercise 2 above.

   • My experience of learning a foreign language
   • The best way to learn another language
   • An example of language change
   • Other languages in your country
   • An aspect of culture that is shown in language

2. Work in small groups. Take turns giving your presentations.

8 | TAKING SKILLS FURTHER

Outside of class, make a list of situations where you hear numbers, for example, in a news report or sports report. How often do you hear approximations in these situations? In the next class, compare your lists.

 For additional listening practice on the topic of language and communication, go to the *Open Forum* Web site (www.oup.com/elt/openforum) and follow the links.

Topic:	Inventors and inventions
Listening Texts:	Conversation with a writer; talk at a technology museum
Listening Skill Focus:	Identifying the purpose of a story or example
Speaking Skill Focus:	Explaining a process
Vocabulary:	Multi-word verbs (1)
Pronunciation:	Word stress

1 INTRODUCING THE TOPIC

1. Work in small groups. Brainstorm what you know about how or when each of the products below was invented. Divide the products into two groups: late nineteenth century inventions and early twentieth century inventions. (Answers are at the bottom of the page.)

	Late nineteenth Century	Early twentieth Century
the automobile		
the telephone		
the television		
the fax machine		
the transistor radio		
the typewriter		
the microwave oven		

2. Work in small groups. Think of three ways that the inventions of the late nineteenth and early twentieth centuries changed people's lives. Compare answers with the whole class.

Answers: late nineteenth century inventions: the automobile, the telephone, the fax machine, the typewriter; early twentieth century inventions: the television, the transistor radio, the microwave oven

2 LISTENING PRACTICE

A Preparing to Listen

Work in pairs. Read the quiz and try to answer the questions.

Inventions Quiz

1. Which of these products was invented by a bank clerk?
   a. photographic film
   b. the automobile
   c. the telephone

2. What household appliance was first known as the radar range?
   a. the transistor radio
   b. the microwave oven
   c. the vacuum cleaner

3. Which means of communication was invented first?
   a. the fax machine
   b. the telephone
   c. the television

4. What office product did not sell for ten years after it came on the market?
   a. the calculator
   b. the photocopy machine
   c. the typewriter

B Listening for Main Ideas

Listen to an interview with the writer of a book about inventions of the late nineteenth and early twentieth centuries. As you listen, check your answers to the quiz above.

C Listening for More Detail

Listen to the interview again. Choose the correct answer to complete each statement. Then compare answers with a partner. Listen again if necessary.

1. The writer is especially interested in _____.
   a. how the inventions were developed
   b. the inventors' personalities
   c. the typewriter and the fax machine

2. Eastman decided to invent photographic materials because _____.
   a. his vacation was canceled
   b. he didn't enjoy his job
   c. his photographic equipment was too heavy to carry

3. Many of the people who invented the new machines were _____.
   a. bank clerks
   b. curious experimenters
   c. professional scientists

4. Percy Spencer discovered that ____.
   a. chocolate melts when you put it in your pocket
   b. popcorn pops in a microwave oven
   c. a magnetron could cause popcorn to pop

5. The fax machine was not a success originally because ____.
   a. it was too difficult to use
   b. people preferred to use the telephone
   c. the telegraph was more popular

6. The typewriter wasn't popular because ____.
   a. letters were supposed to be handwritten
   b. people thought it was too difficult to operate
   c. it didn't work very well

D Focus on the Listening Skill: Identifying the Purpose of a Story or Example

LISTENING SKILL

Speakers often use examples or stories to make a more general point. To identify the purpose of an example or a story, pay attention to how a speaker introduces it, and to how he or she comments on it afterward.

1. Listen again to what the speaker says *before* and *after* the story about George Eastman. Fill in the blanks with the words you hear. Then compare answers with a partner.

   A: A lot of inventors were amateurs, and some of them were considered to be

   nuts . . . crazy! But they had this . . . incredible (1) _____. They (2) _____

   in what they were doing.

   B: Umm.

   A: Take George Eastman, for example . . .

   ————————————————————

   A: So he canceled his vacation, quit his job, stayed home, and invented film instead.

   B: That's great!

   A: The guy was a bank clerk, twenty-four years old! But that was the (3) _____ of

   the time, you know? Talk about a (4) _____! It was a real can-do spirit.

2. Now look at the extract above and choose the correct answer to this question:
   What is the *main reason* that the speaker talks about George Eastman?
   a. To give an example of a determined and confident amateur
   b. To explain how difficult it was to do photography at the time
   c. To show how easy it was for inventors to think of new ideas

3. Listen to the extract, and choose the correct answer. Compare answers with a partner.

   What is the *main reason* that the speaker talks about the microwave oven?
     a. To show how different machines had different uses
     b. To give an example of something that took time to be developed
     c. To give an example of something that was discovered by accident

4. Now listen to this extract, and choose the correct answer. Compare answers with a partner.

   What is the *main reason* that the speaker talks about the typewriter?
     a. To show that Remington is an example of a company that had to spend a lot of money on marketing
     b. To show how people don't always accept a new product immediately
     c. To show how customs were different in the 19th century

E Thinking and Speaking

Discuss the questions in small groups.

   1. What qualities do you think are necessary to become an inventor?

   2. Can you think of three recent inventions? Do you know the names of their inventors?

   3. How do today's inventions change people's lives?

3 VOCABULARY: Multi-Word Verbs (1)

> Multi-word verbs are made up of a verb (*catch, take, go*, etc.) and one or more particles (*on, off, up*, etc.) You can not always guess the meaning of a multi-word verb by looking at the verb and the particle separately.

1. Read these sentences from the interview. Circle three multi-word verbs. Can you guess what they mean?

   People were asking questions. "Hmmm . . . I wonder if we could have a machine that does this?" or, you know . . . "Why can't we do that?" And then they would set out to do it, and they wouldn't give up.

   The French were using very effective fax machines in the 1860s—before the telephone, in fact. But the idea never took off.

2. Each sentence below contains a multi-word verb. Read the sentences. Then on the next page, match each multi-word verb with its definition.

   1. George Eastman didn't like to carry all his photographic equipment, so he **set out** to make the process easier for photographers.

   2. The scientists were determined. They believed in what they were doing, and they never **gave up**.

3. This new vacuum cleaner was last year's most successful product. It **took off** as soon as it entered the market.

4. My alarm clock **goes off** at six o'clock every morning.

5. Do you want to stop now, or should we **go on** until we find a solution?

6. I'm having problems with my computer. Please **come over** and take a look.

7. I'm sorry, but I have to go now. A problem has **come up** at work.

8. How are you **getting along** with your research? Is it going well?

9. The professor finally **turned up** half an hour late.

10. We'll need to finish the project soon. Time is **running out**.

Multi-Word Verb	Definition
_e_ 1. set out	a. to suddenly become popular (a product)
____ 2. give up	b. to make progress
____ 3. take off	c. to continue
____ 4. go off	d. to happen suddenly (a problem)
____ 5. go on	e. to begin a task with an aim or goal
____ 6. come over	f. to arrive or appear
____ 7. come up	g. to stop trying to do something
____ 8. get along	h. to be used up or finished
____ 9. turn up	i. to make a sudden noise
____ 10. run out	j. to visit

3. **Fill in each blank with the correct form of one of the multi-word verbs from exercise 2 above. Then compare answers with a partner.**

1. After trying to fix the photocopy machine all afternoon, I finally _gave up_.

2. We waited for half an hour, but the bus never _____.

3. Kayla Jones was quite well-known locally, but her career really _____ after she recorded the hit song "Go Girl."

4. My best friend _____ to my house last night, and we watched a movie.

5. Julia had to go back to her country because her visa _____.

6. Sorry I'm late. Something _____ at the office, and I couldn't leave earlier.

7. Tom loves his job. He plans to _____ working until he's 70.

8. Many athletes _____ to break a world record, but few actually do.

9. The children are _____ very well in their new school.

10. We had to leave the building because the fire alarm _____.

4. Choose two to four verbs from exercise 2 that are new to you. Write sentences using the verbs. Then compare sentences with a partner.

4 LISTENING PRACTICE

A Preparing to Listen

Work with a partner. Look at the picture of the man and his invention. Discuss the questions.

1. What do you think the machine does?
2. What questions could you ask about the man and/or the invention? (For example, *Why did he invent it?*)

B Listening for Main Ideas

Listen to a guide telling the story of Chester Carlson and his invention. Then choose the best summary.

The story is about _____.
    a. a scientist who made a new discovery by accident
    b. an amateur who believed in his invention
    c. a wealthy man who was generous with his money

C Listening for More Detail

Read through the questions and answer the ones you can. Then listen to the interview again and complete your answers as you listen. Compare answers with a partner.

1. Why was Carlson's invention important?
2. When was the process invented?
3. What kind of childhood did Carlson have?
4. Why did Carlson keep a notebook?
5. Why did he become interested in the duplication process?

6. What was the difficulty that he had at first?

7. When did Haloid agree to develop the machines?

8. When did they sell the first model?

9. What happened when they introduced the first model?

10. What did Chester Carlson do after he became successful?

D Working Out Unknown Vocabulary

 Listen to the extracts from the talk. Listen for the words and expressions in italics below. Choose the correct meaning for each word or expression. Then compare answers with a partner.

1. *Put himself through college* probably means _____.
   a. forced himself to go to college
   b. paid his own college tuition

2. *Duplicate* probably means _____.
   a. copy
   b. print

3. *Turned down* probably means _____.
   a. hired
   b. rejected

4. *Drop it* probably means _____.
   a. give up
   b. invest more money

5. *Modest* probably means _____.
   a. quiet, not showy
   b. proud

E Thinking and Speaking

Discuss the questions in small groups.

1. What kind of person was Chester Carlson?

2. What do you think we can learn from his story?

5 PRONUNCIATION: Word Stress

FYI When the suffixes *-tion, -ic, -ical, -ity, -graphy,* or *-ogy* are added to a noun or a verb, the stress is usually put on the syllable just before the suffix. As a result, adding suffixes to a word sometimes changes the position of the main stress.

1. Listen to these words. Underline the stressed syllable. Then compare answers with a partner.

    1. <u>du</u>plicate   dupli<u>ca</u>tion

    2. imagine   imagination

    3. inspire   inspiration

    4. invent   invention

    5. mechanic   mechanical

    6. technology   technological

    7. photograph   photographic   photography

    8. electric   electrical   electricity

2. Listen again and repeat the words. Circle the pairs of words that have different stress patterns. For example, *duplicate* and *duplication*.

3. Read the sentences. Underline three to five syllables in each sentence that you think will be stressed. Then listen to the recording and check your answers.

    1. <u>Car</u>lson in<u>ven</u>ted an automatic xerographic machine.

    2. The process was called xerography.

    3. His invention used light and electricity to duplicate an image.

    4. Carlson attended the California Institute of Technology.

4. Practice reading the sentences from exercise 3 aloud, using the correct stress.

6 SPEAKING SKILLS: Explaining a Process

SPEAKING SKILL

When you are explaining a process to someone, or showing someone how to operate something, use words and expressions such as the ones in the chart to sequence the explanation and check that the other person understands.

Sequencing	Checking Understanding
Now, . . .	OK?
First, . . .	Is that clear?
Then/Next/After that, . . .	Do you understand?
Finally, . . .	

🎧 1. Listen to the explanation. What kind of machine is the man trying to operate?

🎧 2. Listen again. Which expressions do you hear?

7 | SPEAKING PRACTICE

1. Think of a machine that you often use, or choose one of the machines from the list below. How would you explain to someone how to use it? Divide the process into steps, and make some notes for each step.

   • a microwave oven

   • a camera or video camera

   • an alarm clock (how to set it)

   • a coffee maker or an espresso machine

   • a fax machine

   • a cell phone

2. Work in small groups. Take turns explaining the process to your group. Try to use the expressions from the chart in section 6.

8 | TAKING SKILLS FURTHER

Outside of class, listen to someone giving a lecture or talking. Note whether the person uses a story or an example to make a point. Identify the purpose of the story or example. Is it effective? In the next class, discuss your findings.

 For additional listening practice on the topic of technology, go to the *Open Forum* Web site (www.oup.com/elt/openforum) and follow the links.

CHAPTER **9** Marketing and Advertising

ABOUT THIS CHAPTER

Topic:	Marketing and advertising
Listening Texts:	Listeners' responses to a documentary; informal conversation
Listening Skill Focus:	Summarizing
Speaking Skill Focus:	Checking for understanding
Vocabulary:	Words and expressions related to marketing
Pronunciation:	Using intonation to express interest

1 INTRODUCING THE TOPIC

1. Look at the quiz about advertising. Try to complete it, using the numbers in the box. (The answers are at the bottom of the page.)

$$\boxed{30 \quad 65 \quad 165 \quad 248 \quad 40,000}$$

Advertising Quiz

1. Percentage of local TV news time devoted to advertising:

    _____

2. Amount, in billions of dollars, spent on U.S. advertising in 1999:

    _____

3. Amount, in billions of dollars, spent on U.S. advertising in 2004:

    _____

4. Number of television commercials that the average U.S. child may view in one year:

    _____

5. Percentage of people who believe they are constantly bombarded with too much advertising:

    _____

2. In one minute, list as many different ways of advertising something as you can think of. Then compare lists with a partner. How many different ways did you find?

Answers: 1. 30; 2. 165; 3. 248; 4. 40,000; 5. 65

A Preparing to Listen

Read the statements about advertising, and check the ones that you agree with. Then compare ideas with a partner. Do you have the same opinions?

_____ a. The advertising industry is too powerful.

_____ b. Advertising looks ugly in a natural landscape like a beach or a desert.

_____ c. Children see too many ads for junk food.

_____ d. Advertising should not be aimed at children.

_____ e. Children should learn to evaluate advertisements.

_____ f. Advertising is an important part of our economy.

_____ g. A lot of advertising gives false or misleading information.

_____ h. Young people are so used to advertising that they don't pay any attention to it.

B Listening for Main Ideas

Listen to the responses to a radio program about advertising. Circle on the list above the five opinions that you hear. Then compare answers with a partner.

C Listening for More Detail

Listen to the responses again, and choose the correct answer for each item below. Then compare answers with a partner. Listen again if necessary.

1. Edna Sullivan most dislikes _____.
   a. billboard advertising
   b. advertising on buses
   c. advertisements in natural areas

2. Which one of these points does Robert Bianchi *not* mention?
   a. Advertising helps companies stay in business.
   b. Advertising helps customers decide which products to buy.
   c. Advertising helps keep prices low.

3. Victor Rodriguez doesn't allow his children to watch commercial TV because _____.
   a. they are very young
   b. there are too many commercials
   c. they watch it in school

4. Where do Rodriguez's children see advertisements in school?
   a. On posters and in books
   b. On the school bus
   c. On TV

5. What kind of advertising does Laura Wellman *not* mention?
   a. Ads in school lunches
   b. Ads on the drink machines
   c. Ads on sports clothing

6. What does Sarah Cohen think parents should do?
   a. Believe what their children say about advertising
   b. Limit the amount of advertising that their children see
   c. Teach their children how to react to advertising

D Focus on the Listening Skill: Summarizing

> **LISTENING SKILL**
>
> Summarizing is taking the main points of what you hear and restating them in one or two sentences. Summarizing helps you remember what you heard, check that you have understood, and take notes efficiently.

1. **Listen to Victor Rodriguez's opinion again. After you hear each part, write two to four words *only* in each blank to complete his main points.**

   1. He is shocked at how much marketing is geared toward _young children_.

   2. He can't allow his children to watch _____ because of _____.

   3. He is also concerned about _____.

2. **Now choose the best summary.**

   _____ a. Victor Rodriguez's children are too young to watch TV commercials.

   _____ b. There is too much marketing to young children, both on commercial TV and in school.

   _____ c. Parents should not allow advertisements on TV and in schools.

3. **Listen to Robert Bianchi's opinion. Write two to four words *only* in each blank to summarize the missing information.**

   1. Companies have to _____.

   2. Successful businesses know how to _____.

   3. Without advertising, many companies _____ and we'd pay a lot

      more for _____.

4. Work with a partner. Complete the summary of Bianchi's opinion in no more than two sentences. Then compare summaries with another pair.

Robert Bianchi feels that _____

_____.

E Thinking and Speaking

Choose one of the statements from section A that you feel strongly about. Work in small groups and give your opinions. Then summarize each other's opinions.

3 VOCABULARY: Words and Expressions Related to Marketing

1. Read the paragraphs, paying attention to the words in bold.

When a company decides to invest in a new **product** or **service**, the marketing department usually does **market research** to decide what kind of product is likely to succeed. Marketing executives **conduct surveys** of potential customers. They look at the **competition**: other similar products that are **on the market**. Finally, they decide how to **advertise** the product.

There are many different kinds of advertising. Some products are often advertised on large **billboards** on the roadside for drivers to see. A company might decide to use **TV** or **radio commercials**. They may also use **magazine** or **newspaper** advertise-ments (ads) or advertisements on the **Internet**.

Advertising is usually **geared toward** the type of people most likely to want a particular product. For example, advertisements for a new soft drink may feature rock music, in order to **attract** teenagers. Another popular method is for a company to **sponsor** a popular event, such as a rock concert, in return for free advertising.

2. Fill in the blanks with the correct words in bold from exercise 1.

   1. Before deciding how to advertise, marketing departments _do market research_,

      _____, and _____.

   2. The six different places to advertise that are mentioned in the text are

      _____billboards_____, _____, _____,

      _____, _____, and _____.

3. Complete the sentences with the words in bold from exercise 1.

   1. My sister has her own company: she operates a carpet-cleaning _service_.

   2. There are a lot of people offering the same service. My sister has to make her

      business look better than the _____.

   3. If you have your own business, it's a good idea to _____ in the phone book.

4. Our product isn't doing very well. We ought to do some _____ to find out how we can improve it.

5. What _____ do you use to clean your shower? I can't find one that works.

6. The music festival was canceled because they couldn't find a company to _____ the event.

7. When I watch TV, I always turn down the sound during the _____.

8. If we made the store look nicer, we could _____ a lot more customers.

9. There are several new kinds of candy bars _____ now.

10. The advertisements for soft drinks are _____ young people.

4. **Work in small groups. Discuss how each of the following products is usually advertised. Use as many of the vocabulary words from above as you can.**

- cars
- consumer technology (scanners, cameras, printers, etc.)
- cosmetics and toiletries
- new movies

4 LISTENING PRACTICE

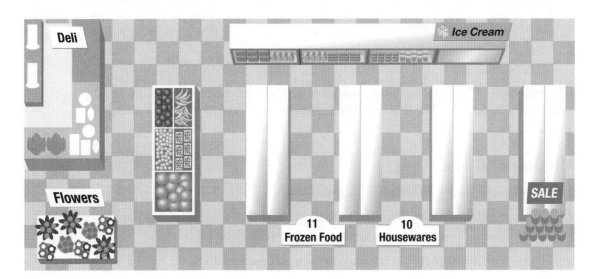

A Preparing to Listen

Discuss the questions in small groups.

1. In your local supermarket, where do you find the following items—at the back of the store, at the front, or in the aisles?
   - candy
   - cleaning products
   - deli (delicatessen) counter
   - milk and dairy products

2. In your opinion, why are products placed where they are?

B Listening for Main Ideas

Listen to a conversation between Sam and Nicole. Check the main point that Nicole is making.

_____ a. It's important to know how to find products in the supermarket.

_____ b. Supermarket products are often placed in inconvenient locations.

_____ c. Products in supermarkets are strategically placed in order to increase sales.

C Listening for More Detail

1. Listen to the conversation again. Fill in the first column of the chart with the items below.

In the aisles   In the front of the store

In back of the store   Around the sides of the store

Near the checkout counters

	Where?	Why?
1. Milk and ice cream	In back of the store	
2. Deli (delicatessen) counter		
3. Bakery		
4. Special offers and free samples		
5. Cleaning products and dog food		
6. Candy		

2. Listen again. In the second column of the chart, note why each product is placed where it is. Then compare answers with a partner.

D Thinking and Speaking

Discuss the questions in small groups.

1. What methods (other than placement) do stores use to get customers to buy things? For example, store window displays, coupons, and so on.

2. Do the different methods affect your shopping and what you buy? If so, how?

3. Which method do you think is the most effective?

4. Think of some advice that you would give a young person to help him or her shop wisely.

5 | PRONUNCIATION: Using Intonation to Express Interest

FYI Intonation is the way your voice goes up and down when you speak. It can help show emotion. For example, when you are interested and enthusiastic, your voice is likely to go up and down more. If you do not use a wide enough range of intonation, you may seem bored or uninterested.

1. Listen to the following short dialogues, paying attention to the intonation in the responses. How interested is the listener? Check the appropriate boxes.

		Not Interested	Very Interested
1.	A: They're going to build a new shopping mall here. B: Really?		
2.	A: Brown's has a really good sale on at the moment. B: I know.		
3.	A: Would you like to see our latest range of carpets? B: Sure.		
4.	A: We can give you 20 percent off if you buy it today. B: Oh.		
5.	A: Are you interested in a cheaper model? B: Yeah.		
6.	A: The jewelry store isn't there any more. B: You're right.		

2. Listen to the dialogues again. Notice and repeat the intonation in the "interested" responses. Then practice all the dialogues with a partner, using "interested" intonation in each response.

6 | SPEAKING SKILLS: Checking for Understanding

SPEAKING SKILL

You can check that you understand a speaker's point by asking for an explanation or by rephrasing what the speaker has said. Use the expressions in the box on the next page.

Asking for an Explanation	Rephrasing
What do you mean?	Oh, you mean . . .
I don't understand.	You're saying that . . .
I don't see what you mean.	So you think . . .
I don't get it.	

1. Listen to the conversation and answer the questions.

   1. What are the people discussing?

   2. What is Susan proposing?

2. Listen to the conversation again. Which expressions from the box above do you hear?

7 | SPEAKING PRACTICE

1. Work in small groups. Choose a product or a service to advertise. Use the ideas in the list, or your own ideas.

   • a new line of designer jeans

   • a "healthy fast-food" restaurant

   • a rock concert in aid of a charity

   • a computer repair service

2. **Make a marketing plan for your product. Use the checklist below to help you. When you are listening to other members of the group, use expressions from section 6 as necessary, to check that you have understood.**

Marketing Plan

Who is the product for? (What is the target market?)

    young/middle-aged/older people

    men/women

    low income/middle income/high income

    people with children/pets/a backyard/a car, etc.

How will you advertise the product?

    on the radio/on TV

    in newspapers or magazines (Which ones?)

    on billboards or posters

    inserts or flyers delivered to the home

    coupons or samples

    at the supermarket or drugstore etc.

When will you advertise it?

    time of day

    day of week

    month or season etc.

What features will you emphasize ? (Choose two or three.)

    style

    convenience

    price

    reliability

    hi-tech etc.

---

3. **Present your plan to the class, and listen to the plans from the other groups. Which plan do you think is the most effective? Why?**

8 | TAKING SKILLS FURTHER

Outside class, observe people talking to each other informally. Listen to how people check that they have understood something. Note the expressions that they use. (Look at facial expressions as well.) Compare your impressions in the next class.

For additional listening practice on the topic of marketing and advertising, go to the *Open Forum* Web site (www.oup.com/elt/openforum) and follow the links.

ABOUT THIS CHAPTER

Topic:	Education
Listening Texts:	Conversation about college credit for life experience; personal experiences of college
Listening Skill Focus:	Identifying opinions and supporting arguments
Speaking Skill Focus:	Using repetition for emphasis
Vocabulary:	Collocations related to education
Pronunciation:	*-ed* vs. *it*

1 INTRODUCING THE TOPIC

1. Work in small groups. In one minute, write down as many different ways as you can think of to learn a new subject or skill.

2. Look at the list of activities below and decide what the best ways to learn them are. Use the ideas in the box or some of your ideas from above. Then compare and discuss answers in small groups.

an intensive class	life experience	private lessons
"teach yourself" books	traditional school	university

1. A foreign language: *an intensive class, private lessons, life experience* _____

2. How to run a business: _____

3. How to play a musical instrument: _____

4. An academic subject (e.g., history): _____

5. How to bring up children: _____

6. How to fix a car: _____

7. How to cook: _____

8. How to use a computer: _____

2 | LISTENING PRACTICE

A Preparing to Listen

Work with a partner. Look back at exercise 2, and discuss the questions.

1. What kinds of activities or subjects are best learned through experience? What kinds are best learned through formal education?

2. How do you think life experience compares with a college education? Is one more important than the other?

B Listening for Main Ideas

1. Listen to a radio commercial for a college. What will Westside College give you credit for?

2. Listen to the conversation about the commercial. Check the three topics that Ben and Mona mention. Do they have the same opinion on the subject?

_____ a. Ways to evaluate life experience

_____ b. Standards for testing and evaluation

_____ c. Kinds of teachers in college

_____ d. Discipline needed to attend college

_____ e. College sports

C Listening for More Detail

Listen to the commercial and the conversation again. For each item, write *T* for true or *F* for false in the blank. Then compare answers with a partner and correct the false statements. Listen again if necessary.

_____ 1. Westside College has three different methods to evaluate previous learning and experience.

_____ 2. Ben says schools have different systems to evaluate previous learning.

_____ 3. Both Ben and Mona are worried that students could falsify documentation of previous learning.

_____ 4. Mona thinks it could be difficult to evaluate extremely different experiences.

_____ 5. Ben feels that the standards for evaluation in college are not completely objective.

_____ 6. Mona feels that life experience takes more discipline than going to college.

_____ 7. Ben says that he started learning more after he finished college.

_____ 8. Ben is thinking about going back to college.

D Focus on the Listening Skill: Identifying Opinions and Supporting Arguments

> **LISTENING SKILL**
>
> When speakers give an opinion, they often also give reasons or examples to support their opinions. When listening to opinions or arguments, try to identify the main opinion and then listen for the supporting reasons or examples. This will help you better understand the entire opinion or argument.

Read the opinions below. Then listen to the extracts from the conversation and write the supporting argument or example that is used in each case. In some cases, there is more than one. Compare answers with a partner. Listen again if necessary.

1. Ben's opinion: *It wouldn't be easy to create false documents.*

   Supporting examples or arguments: _The community college is really strict._

   It's a lot of work to falsify documents.

2. Mona's opinion: *It would be very subjective to evaluate life experience.*

   Supporting example or argument: _____

   _____

3. Mona's opinion: *It seems unfair.*

   Supporting example or argument: _____

   _____

4. Ben's opinion: *Many people say they don't learn a lot in college.*

   Supporting example or argument: _____

   _____

E Thinking and Speaking

1. **Read the statements and make notes about your opinions for each one. Give reasons or examples to support your arguments.**

1. You should be given credit in college for life experience or previous learning.

2. It's a good idea to work for a while before going to a college or university.

3. Good grades in school affect success in life.

2. Work in small groups. Take turns presenting your opinions.

3 | VOCABULARY: Collocations Related to Education

1. Read the advice from a college Web site. Do you agree with all of the advice?

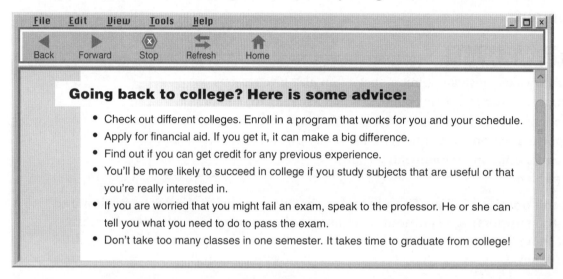

2. Look at the verbs in the first column and note the nouns or phrases they can be used with. Read the Web page in exercise 1 again. Find other nouns or phrases that can be used with each verb.

Verbs	**Nouns/Phrases**
1. apply	to a college/university, for <u>financial aid</u>
2. enroll in	a college/university, _____
3. get	a good/bad grade, a degree, _____, _____
4. study	for a test, _____
5. take	a test, an exam, _____
6. pass	a test, _____, a class
7. fail	a test, _____, a class
8. graduate from	school, _____, a university

3. Complete the sentences with the words from exercise 2. You may have to change the form of some of the nouns or verbs.

1. I enrolled in a <u>program</u> to become an airline mechanic. I took a few

_____, and I got good _____, but then I found out that I had to take calculus, so I changed programs.

2. My cousin Holly _____ from Washington University last June. She

_____ a bachelor's degree.

3. I _____ that class last semester, but I didn't study and I didn't _____

the final exam, so I _____ an F! I'm going to study harder next time.

4. I'd like to go to a four-year college, but the tuition is very expensive. I'll need to

apply for _____. I don't know what I'll do if I don't get it.

4. **Work with a partner. Choose two or three of the following topics, and tell your partner about them.**

- A subject you'd like to study
- The subject you most disliked at school
- A teacher who influenced you
- An important exam you had to take
- A grade you were surprised to get

4 LISTENING PRACTICE

A Preparing to Listen

Work with a partner. Look at the information in the chart, and discuss the questions.

1. Why is the title "The Changing Face of College Students"? How are college students changing?

2. Why do you think these changes are happening?

3. Based on this information, are most college students that you know traditional or nontraditional?

The Changing Face Of College Students

The traditional undergraduate student enrolls in a four-year college straight from high school and studies full-time. Based on that definition, some 73% of undergraduates are in some way nontraditional

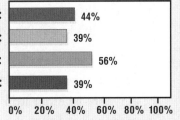

Undergraduates who attend 2-year colleges:	44%
Undergraduates attending school part-time:	39%
Female undergraduate students:	56%
College students (including graduate students) aged 25 or older:	39%

0% 20% 40% 60% 80% 100%

Source: National Center for Education Statistics

B Listening for Main Ideas

Tom   Tracy   Ed   Alicia

Listen to four college graduates talk about their experiences in college. As you listen, match the beginnings and endings of the sentences.

_____ 1. Tom   a. fulfilled a personal dream.

_____ 2. Tracy   b. went to an unusual school.

_____ 3. Ed   c. fulfilled a family's dream.

_____ 4. Alicia   d. discovered an interest that later became a career.

C Listening for More Detail

Listen to the speakers again, and choose the correct answer for each item. Then compare answers with a partner. Listen again if necessary.

Speaker 1: Tom

1. Tom went to a community college first because _____.
   a. it was close to home
   b. his grades weren't very good
   c. he wasn't interested in a four-year college

2. Tom changed his approach to studying after _____.
   a. he found something that interested him
   b. he transferred to a different college
   c. he started his own business

Speaker 2: Tracy

3. Which statement is true about Tracy?
   a. She had a lot of money to pay for school.
   b. She'd always wanted to get a master's degree.
   c. She didn't know if she'd be accepted to Harvard and didn't know how she'd pay for it.

4. Tracy is _____.
   a. certain that she has a better job because of her education
   b. not sure whether it makes a difference that she went to Harvard
   c. disappointed that she didn't go to Harvard for her undergraduate degree, too

Speaker 3: Ed

5. Which statement is *not* true about Ed's school?
   a. Students were expected to participate a lot.
   b. There were no grades.
   c. Students gave grades to other students.

6. At Ed's school, some students _____.
   a. wanted to get a traditional grade such as an A or a B
   b. didn't participate in discussions
   c. disagreed with the written evaluations

Speaker 4: Alicia

7. For Alicia, _____.
   a. school has always been difficult
   b. high school and college were both easy
   c. college was more difficult than high school

8. Writing papers was difficult for Alicia because _____.
   a. she didn't like writing
   b. she had to write them in English, which isn't her first language
   c. she didn't have a computer

D Thinking and Speaking

Work in small groups. Summarize what each person said about his or her college experience. Then discuss the questions.

1. What do you think was the main benefit that each person got from his or her college education?

2. Do you know anyone who has had a similar experience?

5 PRONUNCIATION: *-ed* vs. *it*

1. Read and listen to the sentences. What do you notice about the pronunciation of the words in bold?

   1. When I was in school, I **hated** economics. (verb + *-ed*)
   2. I'm studying economics now, and I **hate it**. (verb + *it*)

2. Read and listen to the sentences. Fill in the blanks with either *wanted* (verb + *-ed*) or *want it* (verb + *it*).

   1. I went back to school because I _____ to do something for myself.

   2. I've made your coffee. Do you _____ now or later?

   3. You can have my cake. I don't _____.

   4. My mother always _____ a large house.

🎧 3. **Listen to the sentences and circle the word(s) you hear.**

1. started/start it
2. started/start it
3. predicted/predict it
4. predicted/predict it
5. repeated/repeat it
6. repeated/repeat it
7. needed/need it
8. needed/need it
9. suggested/suggest it
10. suggested/suggest it

4. **Choose three of the sentences from exercises 1 and 2 above (or make your own). Read the sentences aloud to a partner. See if your partner can identify -ed or it.**

6 SPEAKING SKILLS: Using Repetition for Emphasis

SPEAKING SKILL

Good speakers often use repetition to emphasize a point. This helps the main points stand out more.

🎧 1. **Listen to these three extracts from the recordings. Write the word or phrase that is repeated in each extract. What is the effect of the repetition?**

1. _____

2. _____

3. _____

2. **Work with a partner. Read the descriptions. Emphasize the main point by adding repetition with the underlined words.**

1. I went to a very old-fashioned school. <u>We had to</u> wear a uniform. <u>We had to stand up when the teacher entered the room. We had to ask permission to speak in class.</u>

2. <u>The students</u> made all the decisions at the school. _____
_____

3. Mr. Frank was an <u>unusual</u> teacher. _____
_____

4. Education is <u>important</u>. _____

_____

7 | SPEAKING PRACTICE

1. Think about a positive learning experience that you had during your time in school (elementary, middle, or high) or college, a program that you participated in, a workshop you attended, or any other learning experience. Make notes in the chart, as in the example.

Example:	
Type of experience	Auto shop, in high school
Where and when?	New York, 1995
Why it was good:	The teacher was very clear We had a lot of hands-on experience We learned how to work with tools and how to take care of them Very practical Teacher gave us confidence in our abilities
Any negative points?	There weren't enough tools and sometimes we had to wait a long time to work with a specific tool
General opinion:	It's important for high schools to include practical courses to give kids some work experience

Type of experience	
Where and when?	
Why it was good:	
Any negative points?	
General opinion:	

2. Work with a partner or in small groups. Give a short presentation about your experience. Make sure you include a general opinion about the experience at the end of your talk. Do other people in the class have similar experiences and opinions?

8 | TAKING SKILLS FURTHER

Listen to people talking outside of class. Pay attention to the repetition they use to emphasize points. Choose one example to describe in your next class.

 For additional listening practice on the topic of education, go to the *Open Forum* Web site (www.oup.com/elt/openforum) and follow the links.

ABOUT THIS CHAPTER

Topics:	Moon facts; amateur astronomers
Listening Texts:	Radio call-in program; radio interview about amateur astronomers
Listening Skill Focus:	Identifying key words to understand details
Speaking Skill Focus:	Managing conversation
Vocabulary:	Multi-word verbs (2)
Pronunciation:	Unstressed modal verbs

1 INTRODUCING THE TOPIC

1. Read this short text about Galileo. What was one of his contributions to science?

GALILEO AND THE TELESCOPE

Dutch makers of eyeglasses invented the telescope, but Galileo Galilei (1564–1642) was the first person to use the telescope to study the sky systematically. His telescope was small and not very powerful compared to even a cheap modern telescope, but his discoveries dramatically changed the world's ideas about the universe. He made many contributions to science. Here are a few of his findings:

• The sun had dark spots on it (we now call these sunspots).

• The moon was not smooth, but was covered by mountains and craters.

• The Milky Way galaxy was made up of individual stars.

• There were four moons going around the planet Jupiter.

This last discovery was very significant because it led to understanding that Earth and the other planets in the solar system revolve around the sun. Before that, people believed that the sun and the planets revolved around Earth.

2. Discuss the questions in small groups.

1. How do you think Galileo's discoveries affected the world at the time?

2. In what ways has the study of astronomy or space affected our lives? Do you think there will be any significant discoveries in these areas in the future?

3. What would you like to know more about in the universe?

2 LISTENING PRACTICE

A Preparing to Listen

1. Read these facts about the moon. Five of them are true and one is false. Decide which one is false. (The answers are at the bottom of the page.)

_____ 1. The moon is not round. It is shaped like an egg.

_____ 2. The oldest rock from the moon is 4.5 billion years old.

_____ 3. Scientists are certain about how the moon was formed.

_____ 4. The moon's seas are filled with lava, not water.

_____ 5. Twelve men have walked on the moon.

_____ 6. Astronauts have carried some unusual objects (for example, golf balls) to the moon.

2. Work as a class. Discuss what else you know about the moon.

B Listening for Main Ideas

Listen to a radio call-in show about the moon. Which topics from exercise 1 above are discussed on the show?

C Focus on the Listening Skill: Identifying Key Words to Understand Details

> **LISTENING SKILL**
>
> It is helpful to identify important words, or key words, to help you understand a text. If you identify key words, you can reconstruct what you heard and make sure you have understood.

1. Listen to these extracts from the radio program. For each topic, write down four to eight important words you hear.

   1. water and the moon: _seas, ice, poles, lava_____

   2. formation of the moon: _____

   3. the moon and dinosaurs: _____

2. Compare and discuss answers with a partner. Then, try to put the key words together to reconstruct what you heard.

Answers: 1. T; 2. T; 3. F; 4. T; 5. T; 6. T

3. **Read the extracts below and fill in the blanks with words from exercise 1. Then, listen to the extracts again and add any missing words.**

1. Q: Hi, I'm wondering about water on the moon. Is there actually (1) __water__?

   I've heard about the "seas" on the moon, but are they really filled with water?

   A: That's a good question. They are called (2) __seas__, but they're not filled

   with (3) _____. They're actually filled with (4) _____. The only

   water we know of is in (5) _____ at the poles of the moon.

2. Q: Hello, can you tell me if scientists know how the moon was formed?

   A: That's an interesting one. There have been different (1) _____ on this.

   One theory is that the moon was actually (2) _____ of Earth, but

   it broke off and became (3) _____ in early formation. Another idea

   is that the moon was an object out in space that was "captured" or

   (4) _____ by Earth's gravity—in other words, that it came near

   enough to Earth and then couldn't get away because of (5) _____. And

   then there is the theory that a huge (6) _____ crashed into Earth and

   knocked a large piece of it loose and then this piece formed into the moon.

3. Q: Hi, thanks for taking my call. Did research about the moon help scientists figure

   out how or why (1) _____ disappeared?

   A: There actually is a (2) _____. Scientists studied how craters on the moon

   might have been formed, how something might have (3) _____ into the

   moon and made (4) _____. This research was then used by other

   scientists. They came up with a (5) _____ that a huge (6) _____

   crashing into Earth could have killed all the dinosaurs.

D Thinking and Speaking

Work in pairs. Summarize the questions and answers from the call-in show.
Was any of the information new to you?

3 VOCABULARY: Multi-Word Verbs (2)

1. **Each sentence below contains a multi-word verb. Read each sentence. Then match each multi-word verbs with its definition on the right. Compare your answers in small groups.**

   1. Research about the moon helped scientists **figure out** what happened to dinosaurs.

   2. Some scientists think that the moon **broke off** from the Earth in early formation.

   3. Another theory is that the moon couldn't **get away** from the Earth because of gravity.

   4. Regulations about what astronauts could take into space **came about** because of problems.

   5. They considered every theory because they didn't want to **leave out** any possibility.

   6. The equipment **broke down** so they had to stop the study until they could fix it.

   7. Scientists **came up with** a theory that a huge rock crashing into Earth could have killed all the dinosaurs.

   8. Astronauts need a lot of supplies when they go into space, so they don't **run out of** anything.

   Multi-Word Verb   **Definition**

   _d_ 1. figure out   a. to stop working

   ____ 2. break off   b. to remove part of something by force

   ____ 3. get away   c. to happen

   ____ 4. come about   d. to work out an answer or solution to a problem

   ____ 5. leave out   e. to leave or escape

   ____ 6. break down   f. to not include

   ____ 7. come up with   g. to end or finish the supply of something

   ____ 8. run out of   h. to find or produce a solution, answer, theory or idea

2. **Fill in each blank with the correct form of one of the multi-word verbs from above. Then compare answers with a partner.**

   1. How did this situation _____? We didn't know anything about it.

   2. A part of the tree _____ during the storm. Fortunately, it didn't hit the house.

   3. I'm sorry I'm late. I was in the middle of a meeting and I couldn't _____.

   4. The scientist _____ a great idea to develop a new telescope.

   5. His car _____ so he didn't get home until after 9:00 P.M.

   6. Jen worked on the computer for a long time, but she couldn't _____ what was wrong with it.

7. These instructions don't make sense. I think they _____ some words when they wrote them.

8. Make sure you fill up the gas tank before you leave on the trip. You don't want to _____ gas in the desert!

3. Choose two to four verbs that are new for you, and write sentences using the verbs. Then compare sentences with a partner.

Example:

I couldn't think of a way to remember all the new words in my anatomy class. Then I came up with the idea of recording them onto a CD and listening to them in the car.

4 | LISTENING PRACTICE

A Preparing to Listen

You are going to listen to an interview about amateur astronomers. Read the description of part of the interview. In small groups, discuss what you think the text will tell you about Robert Evans and amateur astronomy.

Astronomy is one of those few fields where amateurs have made significant discoveries. This is unusual because in most other areas of science it is usually professionals, not amateurs, who come up with new theories and make important discoveries. One example of an amateur astronomer who has contributed to the field is Robert Evans.

B Listening for Main Ideas

Listen to the interview. As you listen, note the answers to these questions. Then compare answers with a partner.

1. What does Robert Evans search for?
2. What is his special ability?

C Listening for More Detail

Listen to the interview again. Choose the correct answer for each item. Then compare answers with a partner.

1. According to Sharon Lee, amateur astronomers have made important discoveries related to ____.
   a. the moon and supernovas
   b. comets and supernovas

2. A supernova is a giant dying star that is ____.
   a. bigger than our sun
   b. the same size as our sun

3. Robert Evans has found ____.
   a. 35 or more supernovas
   b. less than 35 supernovas

4. Evans observes the stars from ____.
   a. a special observatory
   b. his house

5. What example does a writer use to describe Evans' ability to memorize patterns of stars?
   a. 1500 handfuls of salt on one table
   b. a handful of salt on each of 1500 tables

6. Compared to professional astronomers observing stars, Evans could ____.
   a. change to different telescopes faster
   b. move his telescope faster

7. Because of new technology that takes thousands of photos of the sky ____.
   a. astronomers have learned more about each supernova
   b. astronomers have found more supernovas

8. Robert Evans ____.
   a. doesn't want to use this technology
   b. wants to use this technology

D Thinking and Speaking

Work with a partner or in small groups. In your own words, summarize what Robert Evans does. Have you heard about anyone else with an extraordinary memory?

5 | PRONUNCIATION: Unstressed Modal Verbs

1. Listen to sentences from the interview. Are the modals (*can, could, will,* and *would*) stressed or unstressed in each case?

2. Listen to these sentences, and fill in the blanks with the modal you hear.

   1. With new technology, astronomers _____ find more supernovas.

   2. Do you think they _____ discover anything new?

   3. What technology _____ help scientists?

   4. It's amazing that he _____ memorize the patterns of the stars.

   5. Do you think you _____ do that?

3. Work with a partner. Practice reading the sentences in exercise 2 with natural stress.

6 | SPEAKING SKILLS: Managing Conversation

SPEAKING SKILL

When people are in a conversation—especially an informal conversation—they often change the topic or move back and forth between topics. The expressions below can help you manage this.

Dealing with Interruptions	Adding Information	Returning to a Topic
If you'll let me come back to that . . .	I want to add/say/mention . . .	Now, back to . . .
I'll get to that in a second.	By the way, . . .	Anyway, . . .
	Let me tell you about . . .	To get back to . . .
	Let me give you an example . . .	As I was saying . . .

1. Listen to this section of the interview again. What topic does Sharon Lee return to?

2. Listen to the extract again. Which expressions from the chart above are used?

7 | SPEAKING PRACTICE

1. Work with a partner. Look at the list of different ways to explore space. What are some possible advantages and disadvantages of each? Which two areas do you think are most worth spending money on? Give reasons for your answers.

Space shuttle

Unmanned space probe

Observatory

Ways to explore space:
- space shuttles
- unmanned space probes
- satellites
- powerful telescopes in space or on Earth
- space observatories on Earth
- space tourism

2. Work in small groups. Discuss your ideas and opinions about space exploration. How similar or different are they? Use expressions from section 6 as necessary.

8 | TAKING SKILLS FURTHER

Outside of class, listen to a talk show or a discussion on a specific topic. Pay attention to changes of topic in the conversation. Note whether you hear any of the expressions in section 6. Discuss your findings in the next class.

For additional listening practice on the topic of astronomy, go to the *Open Forum* Web site (www.oup.com/elt/openforum) and follow the links.

Topic:	Cultural differences
Listening Texts:	Book excerpt about an American living in another country; lecture about culture shock
Listening Skill Focus:	Using paraphrase to work out meaning
Speaking Skill Focus:	Managing a group discussion
Vocabulary:	Expressions related to time and punctuality
Pronunciation:	Linking

1 INTRODUCING THE TOPIC

1. Different cultures have different traditions. For example, people shake hands in the United States, whereas people in Japan bow to each other. What other cultural differences between the United States and other countries can you think of? Work in small groups. Write examples in the chart.

	United States	**Other Countries**
Meeting, greeting, introducing people	shake hands	Japan: bow
Attitudes toward family, older people, and raising children		
School and teaching methods		
Privacy and giving personal information		
Punctuality (being on time and being late)		

2. Work with another group. Compare answers and add to your lists. In which category did you find the most differences between the United States and other cultures?

2 | LISTENING PRACTICE

A Preparing to Listen

You are going to listen to a story about a man from the United States living in another country. In the story, he realizes that he has a different attitude toward punctuality, or being on time, from everyone else. Work with a partner. Discuss how you think the man's attitude might be different.

B Listening for Main Ideas

Look at the questions. Then listen to the story and write your answers.

1. What happened? (Write one sentence.) _____

2. Where did it happen? _____

3. Who did this happen to? _____

C Listening for More Detail

Listen to the story again, and choose the correct answer for each question. Then compare answers with a partner. Listen again if necessary.

1. What was the professor's academic subject?
   a. English
   b. Portuguese
   c. Psychology

2. What kind of difficulties did he expect to have?
   a. Difficulties with language and privacy
   b. Difficulties with time and punctuality
   c. Difficulties with his students

3. Why did he rush to his first class?
   a. He was late.
   b. He thought he was late.
   c. The students were in a hurry.

4. What did he learn from this experience?
   a. Brazilians don't wear watches.
   b. Brazilians argue a lot about what time it is.
   c. Nobody in Brazil seemed to worry about the time.

5. Which sentence is true?
   a. All of the students were late.
   b. Many of the students were late.
   c. A few of the students were late.

6. What do students in California do when a class period is ending?
   a. They start moving their books and looking uncomfortable.
   b. They start screaming.
   c. They leave to go to the bathroom.

7. What did the Brazilian students do at the end of the class?
   a. They left right away.
   b. They stayed to ask questions.
   c. They all stayed until 12:30.

8. What had the class been about?
   a. Statistics
   b. Portuguese
   c. Culture

D Focus on the Listening Skill: Using Paraphrase to Work Out Meaning

> **LISTENING SKILL**
>
> *Paraphrasing* means saying something again, but in different (usually simpler) words. Use paraphrasing to help yourself understand a complex sentence that you have heard or read, or to identify more precisely the parts of a sentence that you do not understand. To paraphrase, break the sentence into parts. Rephrase the parts, using simpler language. Then put the sentence back together.

1. **Read and listen to this extract from the story. Pay attention to the underlined phrases. Then answer the questions.**

   I had just begun an appointment as a visiting professor of psychology at a university in Brazil, near Rio de Janeiro. I arrived <u>anxious to observe</u> just what <u>characteristics</u> of this <u>alien culture would require the greatest readjustment</u> from me.

   1. What does *anxious to observe* mean?

      curious to see, wanting to notice

   2. What does *characteristics* mean?

      things about, aspects of

   3. What does *alien culture* refer to?

      _____

   4. What is *readjustment*?

      _____

2. **Now use your answers from exercise 1 to choose the best paraphrase for the second sentence in the passage.**

   _____ a. When I arrived, I wanted to see what aspects of Brazil I would need to get used to.

   _____ b. When I arrived, I was worried about the way of life at the university.

🎧 3. Listen to this second extract from the story, and answer the questions. Listen again if necessary. Then check your answers with a partner.

1. What difficulties did the man expect? _____

2. What does the expression *It's a piece of cake* mean? What turned out to be a "piece of cake"? _____

3. What is distress? What caused the man more distress? _____

_____

4. Use your answers to the questions in exercise 3 to help you complete the paraphrase of the extract.

He expected _____ but in fact the hardest thing for him

was _____ .

🎧 5. Listen to this third extract and answer the questions. Listen again if necessary. Then check your answers with a partner.

1. Why does the professor never need to look at a clock in California to know when the class hour is ending? _____

2. What is the "shuffling of books"? _____

3. Who has "strained expressions"? What does *strained* mean? _____

_____

4. Are the students really screaming? _____

6. Use your answers to the questions in exercise 5 to help you complete the paraphrase of the extract.

In California, the professor always knows when a class is ending because students

_____ and _____ .

E Thinking and Speaking

The tone of the story is quite humorous. With a partner, discuss which parts of the story you think are the funniest. Where does the humor come from?

3 | VOCABULARY: Expressions Related to Time and Punctuality

1. **Read the paragraphs. Pay attention to the words and expressions in bold.**

> I'm a pretty **punctual** person. When I go to a movie, I like to get there **on time**. I actually prefer to arrive **in time to** get a good seat and buy popcorn. I hate being **in a hurry** and feeling **rushed**. If something is **scheduled to start** at five o'clock **sharp**, I'm always there **ahead of time**. Do you want to know my secret? The clock in my kitchen is **ten minutes fast**!
>
> My brother is the opposite. He's always **running late**. He arrived an hour **late for** Thanksgiving dinner last year, and we started without him. "**It's about time**!" I said when I opened the door. "Where have you been?" "I'm not late!" he protested. "I just didn't want to **waste time** eating turkey when what I really wanted was some pumpkin pie. Now I'm just **in time for** dessert!"

2. **Work with a partner. Divide the words and expressions below into two categories: those to do with punctuality and those to do with lateness. Write them in the chart below.**

ahead of time   behind schedule   early

late for   in a hurry   in time for (an event)

in time to (do something before an event)   on time   "It's about time!"

punctual   running late

Punctuality	Lateness

3. Discuss the questions in small groups. Try to use some of the words and expressions from the previous page.

 1. Are you usually late or on time? How important do you think it is to be on time?

 2. What would you never be late for?

 3. What are you often late for?

 4. How much does it bother you when people are late?

4 | LISTENING PRACTICE

A | Preparing to Listen

1. You are going to listen to a lecture about culture shock. Before you listen, read the following definition of this term from the Oxford Dictionary of American English:

   culture shock *(noun)* a feeling of confusion etc. that you may experience when you go to a country that is very different from your own

2. Work in small groups. Discuss the following questions:

   1. What kind of people do,you think might suffer from culture shock?

   2. In addition to confusion, what feelings do you think might be associated with culture shock?

   3. Why is it important to learn about culture shock?

B | Listening for Main Ideas

Listen to the lecture. Number the stages of culture shock 1 through 5. Then compare answers with a partner. Discuss what you remember about each stage.

_____ a. the rejection stage

_____ b. reverse culture shock

_____ c. the adjustment stage

_____ d. the honeymoon stage

_____ e. the superiority stage

C Listening for More Detail

Listen to the lecture again. As you listen, fill in the notes. For items 4–7, provide one to three examples of what happens at each stage. Then compare answers with a partner. Listen again if necessary.

Culture Shock

1. Definition: _____

2. Expression Invented in: _____

3. Honeymoon Stage: Its' exciting/fun. Feel like a tourist _____

4. Rejection stage: _____

5. Superiority stage: _____

6. Adjustment stage: _____

7. Reverse culture shock: _____

8. Important to know about culture shock because: _____

D Working Out Unknown Vocabulary

Listen to the extracts from the lecture. Listen for the words and expressions in italics below. Choose the correct meaning for each word or expression. Then compare answers with a partner.

1. *Euphoric* probably means _____.
   a. happy, positive
   b. frightening, scary

2. *Go out of their way* probably means _____.
   a. travel a long way
   b. take extra trouble

3. *Come to terms with* probably means _____.
   a. learn to deal with
   b. begin to enjoy

4. *A fish out of water* probably means _____.
   a. someone in unfamiliar surroundings
   b. someone who is going to die

5. *Fed up with* probably means _____.
   a. full of
   b. bored or unhappy with

6. *Romanticizing* probably means _____.
   a. making something seem better than it is
   b. making something seem worse than it is

E Thinking and Speaking

Have you ever experienced any of the stages of culture shock described in the lecture? If not, do you know anyone who has? Work in small groups. Describe the experience, and see if the group can identify the stage.

5 PRONUNCIATION: Linking

When a word that ends in a consonant sound is followed by one beginning with a vowel sound, English speakers often link them by running them together without a break between words. This is a natural feature of spoken language, but it can make it hard to hear the boundaries between words.

1. Listen to the sentences and notice how the words are linked. How do you think this affects listening?

   We're ‿ out ‿ of it.
   It ‿ all ‿ adds ‿ up.
   We turned ‿ it ‿ off.

2. Repeat the sentences yourself, linking the words together as the speaker does.

3. Listen to the sentences and write the missing words in the blanks.

   1. At _first it was a_____ positive experience.

   2. I _____ England.

   3. I _____ account.

   4. But I _____ job.

   5. In the end, I _____ .

   6. But it _____ .

4. Listen to the sentences again and mark where a word ending in a consonant sound links to a word beginning with a vowel sound. Then practice saying the sentences, linking the words appropriately.

6 SPEAKING SKILLS: Managing a Group Discussion

When taking part in a discussion, use the phrases in the chart below to ask people for suggestions, confirm agreement, or move from one discussion topic to the next.

Asking for Suggestions	Asking for More Suggestions	Confirming Agreement	Moving to the Next Point
What do you think?	Any other ideas?	Are we all clear about . . . ?	Let's go to the next point.
What could we put down here?	What else could we say?	Do we all agree that . . . ?	Can we move on?
	Does anyone have anything to add to that?		Let's move on.

 1. Listen to the conversation. What are the people discussing?

 2. Listen again. Notice how the leader of the group manages the brainstorming session. Which expressions do you hear?

7 | SPEAKING PRACTICE

1. Work in small groups. Brainstorm some advice for a friend who is going to work overseas. Make a list of specific things that the person can do to minimize the effects of culture shock. (Use the categories on the next page to help you, or add your own.) Try to use some of the expressions from the chart above to manage the discussion.

> *Before you leave: read about the culture, learn some of the language, meet people*
>
> When you arrive: _____
>
> Language: Ask for help with the new language _____
>
> Job: _____
>
> Friends and social life: _____
>
> Free time: _____
>
> Communicating with people at home: _____
>
> _____

2. Compare your answers as a class. Which suggestions do you think are the most useful?

8 | TAKING SKILLS FURTHER

Next time you are participating in a group discussion outside of class, notice how people manage the discussion. Note the expressions that they use. What other ways do people use to manage a discussion? Share your findings in the next class.

 For additional listening practice on the topic of culture shock, go to the *Open Forum* Web site (www.oup.com/elt/openforum) and follow the links.